YOUR KNOWLEDGE HAS VALUE

- We will publish your bachelor's and master's thesis, essays and papers

- Your own eBook and book - sold worldwide in all relevant shops

- Earn money with each sale

Upload your text at www.GRIN.com
and publish for free

Bibliographic information published by the German National Library:

The German National Library lists this publication in the National Bibliography; detailed bibliographic data are available on the Internet at http://dnb.dnb.de .

Imprint:

Copyright © 2017 GRIN Verlag
Print and binding: Books on Demand GmbH, Norderstedt Germany
ISBN: 9783668872943

This book at GRIN:

https://www.grin.com/document/452617

Dr. Khalid Khan

Towards Efficient Resource Allocation in Desktop Grid Systems

Inherent Problems and Traditional Solutions

GRIN Verlag

GRIN - Your knowledge has value

Since its foundation in 1998, GRIN has specialized in publishing academic texts by students, college teachers and other academics as e-book and printed book. The website www.grin.com is an ideal platform for presenting term papers, final papers, scientific essays, dissertations and specialist books.

Visit us on the internet:

http://www.grin.com/

http://www.facebook.com/grincom

http://www.twitter.com/grin_com

Towards Efficient Resource Allocation in Desktop Grid Systems

Dr. Muhammad Khalid Khan

Director

College of Computing and Information Sciences

PAF Karachi Institute of Economics and Technology,

Karachi, Pakistan

Preface

Desktop grid systems are one of the largest paradigms of distributed computing in the world. The idea is to use the idle and underutilized processing cycles and memory of the desktop machines to support large scale computation. The design issues in desktop grid systems are much more complex as compared to traditional grid environment because the hosts (desktop machines) participating in the computation do not work under one administrative control and can become unavailable at any point in time. The heterogeneity and volatility of computing resources, for example, diversity of memory, processors, and hardware architectures also play its role. To get fruitful results from such hostile environment, scheduling tasks to better hosts become one of the most important issues. The work presented in this book focuses on the issue of task scheduling and resource allocation in desktop grid systems and presents concrete contributions.

The main contribution of this work is about minimizing the applications turnaround time on desktop grid systems that can only be achieved through knowledgeable task scheduling mechanism. A Group based Fault Tolerant Scheduling and Replication Mechanism (labeled as GFTSRM) is proposed that uses collective impact of CPU and RAM, task completion history and spot checking to populate available hosts in relevant groups to perform group based task scheduling. It is shown that grouping the hosts on the basis of computing strength and behavior is necessary for better performance. Relevant replication strategies are appended to each group in order to reduce the wastage of processing cycles. Simulations are performed by using GFTSRM, FCFS (First Come First Serve) and PRI-CR-Excl (host exclusion based on the fixed threshold of clock rate). GFTSRM is compared with FCFS because it is the most commonly used task scheduling mechanism. PRI-CR-Excl is used for comparison with the proposed group based scheduling mechanism that takes into account "collective impact of CPU and RAM" while on the contrary PRI-CR-Excl excludes hosts on the fixed threshold of clock rate. The simulation results show that GFTSRM reduces the application turnaround time by more than 35% as compared to FCFS. The proposed group based scheduling mechanism also depicted improvement of more than 20% on application completion time as compared to PRI-CR-Excl.

Table of Contents

List of Figures

List of Tables

1. Introduction

There was a time when super computers were the only option for high-end computing and storage. These days, desktop grid systems have developed into more cost-effective substitutes. There is an abundance of available bandwidth for communication and desktop grids use it thoroughly for the utilization of idle processing cycles and memory of millions of computers connected through Internet or any other type of network. This has given power to decompose computationally infeasible problems into smaller problems, distribute smaller problems to the host/volunteer computers, and aggregate results from volunteers to form solutions to large-scaled problems.

Desktop grid systems can be divided into two categories [115]*. When the computers of an enterprise are used to increase the turnaround time of a compute intensive application, it is called *enterprise wide desktop grid* or simply *desktop grid*. The other category is *volunteer computing* in which home and enterprise computers take part by volunteering idle processing cycles to achieve high throughput. The desktop grid system infrastructure consists of N number of desktop machines in which one would be termed as *master* and the others would be known as *hosts/workers* as shown in Figure 1. Practically, a desktop grid system project has several servers to create tasks, distribute them, record the tasks and corresponding results, and finally, aggregate the results of a set of tasks. The tasks and corresponding work units (evaluating data sets) are distributed by the server to the hosts (client installed computer), typically through a software which permits people to participate in the project. Normally, when a host is idle (i.e., the computer's screensaver is running), then it is the time to work on the tasks assigned by server. After finishing the tasks, the results are sent to the server. In case the computer that is running a client gets busy

References are given in alphabetical order

again, then the client pauses the processing immediately so that the user can execute its own programs. The client continues processing the tasks as soon as the computer becomes idle again.

Desktop grid system frameworks simplify and automate various functions performed by master and client. Master is responsible for user and job management, client management, task management, results verification, security and performance management. Whereas, the client is responsible for collection of hardware statistics from machine, requesting and collecting tasks, task execution, sending back results and allowing users to set preferences. Some of the more popular desktop grid systems frameworks are BOINC [6], OurGrid (peer-to-peer) [89], XtremWeb [26], SZTAKI Desktop Grid [110], and HT Condor [38].

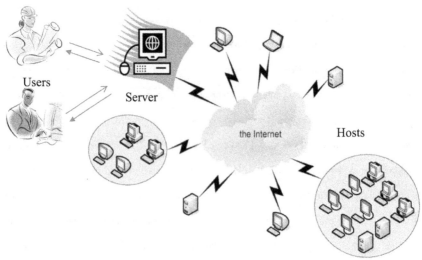

Figure 1: Infrastructure of Desktop Grid Systems
Source: Author's own work

Moreover, the phenomena that has started from the PARC Worm (Xerox's initiative to develop worms to enable distributed computing) [106] has resulted in various successful implementations such as SETI@home [104], GIMPS [35], Folding@Home [87], FightAidsAtHome [27], Computing Against Cancer [14], Einstein@home [22]. These projects have taken up various scientific problems that include searching for cures of diseases, looking for evidence of extraterrestrial intelligence, finding Mersenne prime numbers, and solving several encryption challenges. Apart from the scientific projects, desktop grid systems have gathered recognition also at corporate level. The business enterprises are inspired with the huge success of desktop grid systems. As there is an abundance of desktop resources in such enterprises, it seems a very cost effective solution to utilize the idle processing cycles of such systems and achieve high-end computing. Various such projects have been launched by academia [8, 26, 90, 102, 30] and industry [11, 93, 18].

Notwithstanding their use, there are certain limitations to desktop grid systems which include resource management, scheduling, verification of results, computation time, fault tolerance, security breaches, connectivity and bandwidth issues. The nodes in a desktop grid system environment are inherently volatile, can be heterogeneous, are slower than high-end machines, and the communication mechanism doesn't guarantee five nine reliability. The fact that nodes may fail at any time arises various design and deployment challenges.

Moreover, there is a difference in perspective to scheduling policies as per the needs of scientists and volunteers. Although these perspectives are somewhat contradictory to each other but the scheduling policy should adhere to the needs of both stakeholders. For example, the scientist would like to verify the results and would not mind investing processing cycles for it, whereas the volunteer would like to spend more time on actual processing and would count verification as wastage of resources. These requirements of scientists and volunteers are shown in Figure 2.

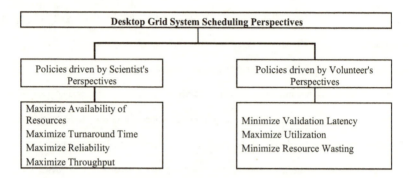

Figure 2: Classification of Scheduling Perspectives in Desktop Grid Systems
Source: Author's own work

Moreover, different scheduling policies are implemented in a typical desktop grid system that can be broadly categorized into the following three categories as shown in Figure 3: [In figure 3 and 4, bracketed numbers are the references]

- A *server scheduling policy* takes care of tasks assignment to server and is based on clients and tasks preferences (for example size of the job, speed of the host, particular operating system, amount of disk space etc). A scoring-based scheduling policy assigns values to individual parameters which are used to calculate the overall impact.

- A *CPU scheduling policy* is related to CPU scheduling of desktop grid application's tasks (works on top of the local operating system's scheduler) and addresses issues such as the particular task to be executed from the currently run-able tasks, and the particular task to be kept in memory from the list of preempted tasks.

- A *work fetch policy* determines when a client can ask for more work and the amount of work that can be requested by a client.

Scheduling policies can also be classified as *naive* or *adaptive* as shown in Figure 4. The naive scheduling policies do not consider any historical knowledge whereas adaptive scheduling policies use a knowledge-base having historical information and threshold values.

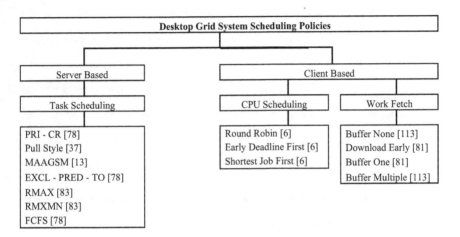

Figure 3: Classification of Task and CPU Scheduling Policies and Work Fetch Policies
Source: Author's own work

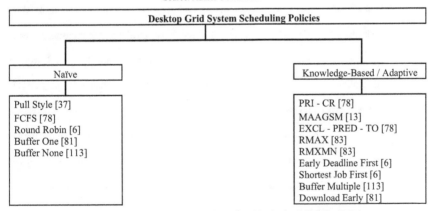

Figure 4: Classification of Naïve and Knowledge-based / Adaptive Scheduling Policies
Source: Author's own work

Moreover, the scheduling policies should strive to attain fault tolerance and result verification. This is done through various mechanisms such as *replication*, *voting* and *spot checking*. In replication, similar tasks are assigned to multiple volunteers to counter the problem of volunteer's unavailability that can be categorized into *host unavailability* and *CPU unavailability*. Replication coupled with voting is used for result verification. In voting, results from multiple volunteers being assigned the same task are compared and the result submitted by the majority of the volunteers is counted as correct. Spot checking is done to assess the reliability of the volunteer. In spot checking, a spot job is submitted to the volunteer whose result is already known to the server. Fault tolerance has its own issues; if not done properly, the overhead generated by the fault tolerant mechanism can increase the wastage of processing cycles.

The work presented in this thesis, attempts to address the aforementioned diversity and requirements of task scheduling/ resource allocation process in desktop grid systems. The thesis presents concrete contributions in two separate areas, described below:

- **Group based Fault Tolerant Scheduling and Replication Mechanism for Desktop Grids:** After the thorough evaluation of the traditional scheduling mechanisms presented in the literature, research gaps are identified and a Group based Fault Tolerant Scheduling and Replication Mechanism (GFTSRM) is proposed that uses collective impact of CPU and RAM, task completion history and spot checking to populate available hosts in relevant groups to perform group based task scheduling. Different replication strategies are also appended with the proposed scheduling mechanism to reduce wastage of processing cycles. The aim of the proposed mechanism is to reduce the applications' turnaround time in desktop grid systems.

- **Predictive Analytics in Desktop Grid Scheduling:** The use of Predictive Analytics (PA) technology to predict host availability in desktop grids is investigated, which is one of the research direction adopted by current desktop grid researchers. After establishing the research gap, a detailed investigative process is implemented which applies a set of state-of-the-art PA techniques to predict availability, with the intent of discovering a type of roadmap for PA application to desktop grid domain. For this, the predictive problem is casted as both a classification and regression process. Moreover, the impact on predictive performance of using different thresholds of availability in the classification process is investigated.

These two areas are elaborated separately in coming sections.

1.1. Group based Fault Tolerant Scheduling and Replication Mechanism for Desktop Grids

As stated earlier, the naive scheduling policies do not consider volunteer's availability and reliability as decision making factors because these polices do not work on historical information. Hence the task assignments to volunteers remain arbitrary. Although these policies such as First Come First Server (FCFS) are easy to design and implement and are used by many volunteer computing platforms, they do not guarantee results. On the other hand, the knowledge based / adaptive policies consider historical information and are capable to adapt to changing circumstances. These policies consider hardware parameters, reliability and availability as decision making parameter but are complex, require additional processing cycles and time for processing.

Researchers have come up with different strategies for resource scheduling in desktop grid environment. To quote some examples, in [37], resources are selected and eliminated for task assignment according to the clock rates and task completion prediction. Moreover, Choi et. al. presented a grouping mechanism in [13], which is based on volunteer autonomy failure, availability and service time. The volunteer groups in this mechanism are managed through mobile agents. These agents are responsible for scheduling task as per the directives of server. Also, in [78], the volunteer's availability is classified into host availability and CPU availability. Host availability reflects that the volunteer is connected with volunteer computing environment whereas, CPU availability shows that volunteer is connected with volunteer computing environment and its idle cycles are available for task performance in volunteer environment. Kondo et. al. presented a replication mechanism in [81], which is based on volunteer grouping but the grouping itself is just based on the hardware strength which is not the right criteria.

In [77], the author arranged the volunteers in two classes i.e., conservative and extreme, by emphasizing their location and network, where location refers to home and/or work place. It is concluded that conservative volunteers having low bandwidth are 90% idle whereas, extreme volunteers, i.e., workplace volunteers, are 80% idle having relatively high bandwidth than conservative volunteers. Furthermore, in [3], Anderson et. al. have studied the effects of volunteer's hardware resources like CPU, RAM, and storage along with network bandwidth, on volunteer computing projects. It is concluded that the evaluation of hardware resources individually is not appropriate because higher disk space plays its role, if proper network bandwidth is available to access it. Similarly, higher processor speed could positively affect processing if more RAM is available to it.

In [101], it is concluded that replication with majority voting is the most reliable sabotage tolerance method in order to achieve a host error rate of 1×10^{-5}. In [37], hosts are categorized as reliable and semi-reliable according to their communication and computation capabilities and then on the basis of these factors job batches are assigned to hosts. Moreover, Watanabe et. al. proposed a mechanism in [116] to reduce the overhead occur as a result of spot-checking which in turn reduces the computation time in volunteer computing environment. However, extra emphasis on replication can waste the CPU cycles. Finally, in [113], Toth et. al. investigated the effects of task retrieval policies such as *buffer none, buffer one,* and *buffer some* on task completion. These policies are to be executed on the host getting the work from the desktop grid application. It is concluded that the effect of task retrieval policies have direct impact on the processing. Some concrete observations from the aforementioned literature survey are:

- Elimination of workers on the basis of hardware strength is not feasible because a worker that possesses less hardware capability may provide more processing time and/or its hardware strength may get better.

- Replication is good for fault tolerance but the excessive replication may result in wastage of processing cycles.

- To evaluate the reliability, spot checking is necessary but spot checking also consumes precious processing cycles.

- Delayed correct results and erroneous results also cause wastage of CPU cycles.

- The task assignment to arbitrary hosts may result in task failure due to host and CPU unavailability or slow processing capability.

Moreover, the author is unable to find any work that takes into account computing ability, reliability as well as availability as a decision making criteria for scheduling in desktop grids.

Researchers have used either hardware parameters or availability as decision making criteria. Though group based scheduling mechanisms have been proposed earlier, the criteria for group allocation have either been host behavior or hardware resources. There is no mechanism that groups the hosts of the basis of collective impact of hardware resources (CPU and RAM), availability (Task Completion History) and also performs reliability checking (spot checking). Moreover, a scheduling mechanism should be fault tolerant and researchers have proposed various replication strategies to achieve fault tolerance. As excessive replication can cause wastage of precious processing cycles, it should be performed only when required. Limited work has been done in this area. Researchers have proposed few optimized replication strategies but these mechanisms are appended with poor scheduling mechanisms; hence, the required results remained out of reach. Similar to replications, excessive spot checking also causes wastage of processing cycles. Spot checking is required to validate the results and to assess the host's reliability. Though an optimized spot checking mechanism is proposed in [116], it requires complex calculations; hence, consumes a high frequency of processing cycles. There is no scheduling mechanism that incorporates a smart and less resource hungry spot checking mechanism.

Based on the above discussion, three research questions have been developed:

- What is the impact of combining computing ability, reliability and availability on the applications turnaround time in desktop grid systems?
- What is the impact of grouping similar volunteers on scheduling in desktop grid systems?
- What is the impact of grouping similar volunteers on replication in desktop grid systems?

To answer these questions, a mechanism for desktop grid systems called Group based Fault Tolerant Scheduling and Replication Mechanism (GFTSRM) is proposed, with an aim to improve the replication and knowledgeable task scheduling that results in the reduction of application's turnaround time. The idea is to group the volunteers on such criteria that can help in achieving more knowledgeable task allocation. GFTSRM categorizes hosts in three groups on the basis of *"collective impact of CPU and RAM"*, *"spot checking"* and *"task completion history"*. It performs task scheduling by giving priority to hosts belonging to more reliable group. GFTSRM also offers different replication techniques, i.e., proactive, reactive and hybrid for each group. This group based scheduling mechanism is the backbone of the GFTSRM. When a host logs on to a project, its "collective impact of CPU and RAM" is calculated and recorded in database. The next step is to spot-check the host. If the host is unable to clear the spot check thrice, it is marked as saboteur. For non-saboteur hosts, past history of task completion will be evaluated and recorded in the database which will be utilized by procedure that assigns individual hosts to a group. In this work, three pre-defined groups are used with titles *Platinum, Gold* and *Silver*. Volunteers are assigned to these groups by using three measures, i.e., collective impact of CPU and RAM, spot checking and task completion history. Group assignment is a cyclic process and can also take place on worker's task request. When the host sends back the result of assigned task within the deadline, the result is recorded in the database. This also updates the record of percentage of task completed on time for that particular host.

The proposed mechanism is evaluated over 90 nodes by using trace driven simulation. The traces were gathered from 90 actual hosts executing compute intensive jobs. Hosts are individually managed by their owners and have variation in computing resources and usage pattern. These hosts are also volatile because they only take part in desktop grid system project when their CPU cycles are idle. When a host becomes available to desktop grid system project, it acknowledges the server through desktop grid system client software. Host is assigned task from the server after availability acknowledgement. During execution, if hosts' CPU becomes unavailable, then the task stops but resumes again when the hosts' CPU becomes available. If host gets powered off, then the task will restart rather resume (checkpoint is not considered in this work, that allows the task's state be saved and allows the task to be resumed rather than restart).

By focusing on grouping mechanism, replication is optimized. Three replication mechanisms are considered in this work. In proactive replication, replica of every task is created at the time of actual task assignment, whereas in reactive replication, replica is only created when the task is delayed. In hybrid replication, replica is created when the task has a risk of delay. In the proposed mechanism, reactive, proactive and hybrid replication mechanisms are used for platinum, silver and gold group's respectively because the volatility of hosts decreases from platinum to silver group.

GFTSRM results are compared with FCFS which simply schedules jobs on first come first server basis and used by most volunteer computing system in recent time [78]. In addition to FCFS, PRI-CR-Excl [78] is also used for comparison purpose which excludes hosts on the basis of fixed clock rates. PRI-CR-Excl is used for comparison because GFTSRM excludes hosts on the basis of "collective impact of CPU and RAM". It is shown that the appropriate scheduling and replication mechanisms can only be implemented after the grouping of resources on computing strength and behavior. GFTSRM ensured that tasks are allocated to hosts with higher probability of tasks completion that resulted in the minimization of tasks failures, improvement in fault tolerance and reduction of application's turnaround time of desktop grid system projects.

The results show that more knowledgeable heuristics can result in task assignment to better host that results in improved application's turnaround time. This also confirms that each criterion has its own importance in decision making. Grouping similar hosts helps in scheduling as once the groups are populated resource allocation can be done on arbitrary basis for some time. Moreover, grouping similar hosts also helps in optimizing replication as relevant replication strategies can be applied to the hosts belonging to same group on the basis of group's reliability index. Hence the level of replication can be lowered down.

1.2. Major Contributions

Following are the major contributions of the thesis:

1. Proposed a host selection mechanism based on the collective impact of processing cycles and memory that proved better than eliminating host on the basis of single hardware parameter such as clock rate.

2. Proposed a group based task scheduling mechanism that is based upon spot checking, task completion history and collective impact of processing cycles and memory. Results suggest that the proposed mechanism outperformed the most widely used naïve scheduling mechanism, i.e., FCFS (first come first serve).

3. Identified the best suited replication mechanism for each group that reduced the replication and minimized the wastage of processing cycles.

1.3. Potential Benefits of Research

Recent years have witnessed a drastic drop in the personal computer prices that has resulted in the high sale these computers. In addition, many students have their own computers and all universities and colleges have computers laboratories and libraries. Almost all of these computers are connected to the Internet and usually remain powered on for the whole day. Although used for some percent of the time, these computers sits idle for most of the day. The potential of using these computers during idle periods is really high. It is expected that the idle processing cycles will only grow in the future because the number of computer would definitely increase. The availability of multi-core processors has also started to make their presence felt and in future, may facilitate the utilization of idle processing cycles.

The motivation of this thesis work is based on the potential benefits to society that can be realized by desktop grid system projects. As the awareness of desktop grid systems has increased, more projects are coming in this arena related to finding cures of diseases such as AIDS and cancer that could improve the quality of life for millions of people. It is quite clear that the effort to increase the overall performance of desktop grid system is a worthwhile goal.

The second motivating factor is related to improve the application's turnaround time. Although many idle computing cycles have been harnessed, a limited number of people participate in such projects. In fact, less than 1% of an estimated 300 million Internet-connected personal computers participate in desktop grid projects [113]. As the number of projects is increasing, the requirement of idle CPU cycles is also increasing. Unless the running desktop grid projects are complete, the new projects are not likely to get idle CPU cycles so there is a need to improve the application's turnaround time. The proposed Group based Fault Tolerant Scheduling and Replication Mechanism provides inroads in this direction. The suggested improvements can potentially serve to boost the trust and confidence of the people in desktop grids.

Moreover, organizations in third-world countries like Pakistan typically do not have abundance of computing infrastructure, as IT is still counted as an expense rather than investment. The economic activity of the country is also substantially dependent on the small and medium enterprises having even worse IT infrastructure due to weak financial footings. It is hence critical to work on desktop grid systems platform that would enable these organizations to use their weak existing IT infrastructure for high end analytical processing, such as analysis of sales to estimate future trends etc. As the organizations, especially SMEs, start to get the analytical processing results from their own infrastructure, it helps in establishing trust on the use of IT for better profitability than one could expect higher investments and more dependence on information systems from these organizations that may be the starting point of an IT revolution in SMEs.

The thesis is organized in the given fashion. Chapter 2 presents the necessary background of distributed computing in general and desktop grid systems in particular. It also highlights scheduling issues in desktop grid environment and associated challenges. Chapters 3 discusses the related work and also suggests taxonomy of published work in the given areas. Chapter 4 presents the methodology of the proposed mechanism i.e. GFTSRM and Chapter 5 discusses the experimental setup and results of GFTSRM. Chapter 7 concludes the thesis whereas, chapter 8 and 9 present future work and references respectively.

2. Background

The aim of this chapter is to introduce the concepts that are discussed in the subsequent chapters of the thesis. The chapter starts by giving a short introduction of distributed computing and its popular variants. Then the scheduling issues in a typical distributed computing environment are highlighted, followed by a detailed discussion on the desktop grid systems. Some famous desktop gird system frameworks and projects are introduced. To close the discussion of this area, the design issues of desktop grid systems related to scheduling in such volatile environment are discussed. Next, predictive analytics is introduced in detail that also highlights the predictive process. At the end, discussion is carried out on the predictive analytics algorithms used in the thesis experiments, namely *k*-Nearest Neighbour, Naïve Bayes, Random Forest, Multi-Layer Perceptron, LibSVM library, Multiple Linear Regression, and Polynomial Regression.

2.1. Distributed Computing

A Distributed Computing System (DCS) consists of disjoint memory and multiple processors that are connected through some sort of communication mechanism [111]. For a user, the overall system appears as one system and it is the system's responsibility to distribute computational modules of the given task to the required processing nodes to achieve efficient execution. The advancements in communication technologies have enabled the connectivity of various computational and informational resources dispersed over a wide geographical area.

A computational task consists of various modules, and scheduling of executable modules over the appropriate computing nodes becomes a mandatory requirement to achieve good turnaround. The parallelism achieved in this way ensures higher performance, lower cost and sustained productivity in real-life applications [108]. Thus, distributed processing can be viewed as a form of parallel processing in a specialized environment. Distributed computing results in resource multiplicity and system transparency that helps in incremental growth, i.e., the power of a DCS can be extended by simply adding additional resources.

Realizing the potential of distributed computing, people started to use the processing cycles of machines available over local area networks, which lead to different types of distributed computing paradigms including the cycle-stealing paradigm in which idle computers available over a network are asked to work on tasks, thus "stealing" the unproductive CPU cycles. Various middleware are available through which people can submit tasks to a central computer that assigns submitted tasks to a group of computers having idle processing cycles. Cluster computing, grid computing, cloud computing and desktop grid computing can be covered under the umbrella of distributed computing.

Cluster computing refers to a group of computers connected by a network under one administrative domain. However, each computer is used by different people [94]. Clusters are used for computation intensive tasks that cannot be performed on a single system or take too long on single system. Cluster may contain different types of computers. Although it is not necessary that all the nodes in a cluster work on the same application, the power of a cluster is to enable individual nodes to work on a portion of a single application that results in performance comparable to a supercomputer. As compared to supercomputer, a cluster is composed of ordinary computers and additional nodes can be added to clusters at any point. Supercomputers may contain thousands of processors and terabytes of RAM. Similar to a cluster, a supercomputer's processors can work on many smaller tasks assigned to them from a single application. However, having supercomputer means, one machine needs to be managed whereas in cluster, many separate computers must be managed. Figure 5 depicts a typical cluster environment.

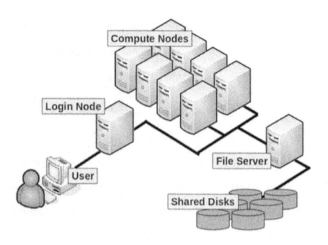

Figure 5: Cluster Computing Concept Diagram (adapted from [65])

When computer resources from multiple administrative domains work together to reach a common goal, this is called *grid computing* [94]. Grids usually involve non-interactive workloads that involve a large number of files. As compared to clusters, grids are more loosely coupled, heterogeneous, and geographically dispersed. It is common to use a single grid for variety of applications. Grid can also be thought of a "super virtual computer" composed of many loosely coupled computers connected via various forms of communication mechanism to perform very large tasks as shown in Figure 6. The term "Grid" was launched by Dr. I. Foster in the latter half of 1990's [94]. According to Foster, Grid should possess the following criteria [29]:

- The resources should not be in the control of a single firm or company.

- A grid uses "standard, open, general-purpose protocols and interfaces".

- A grid delivers "nontrivial qualities of service".

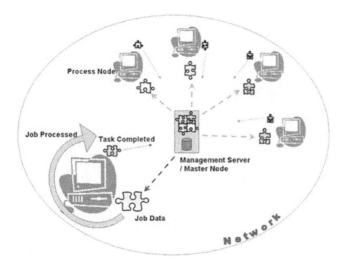

Figure 6: Grid Computing Concept Diagram (adapted from [52])

Besides this, *Cloud computing* refers to the engagement of a large number of computational resource typically connected through internet [5]. It focuses on economically sharing of internet based resources by delivering computing as a service rather than as a product. The computing resources may include applications, platforms and infrastructure as shown in Figure 7. Cloud resources are charged on subscription-based or pay-per-use models. These resources can be re-allocated to other users as per need. The concept of cloud computing has given a way to increase computing capabilities on the fly to extend existing IT capabilities.

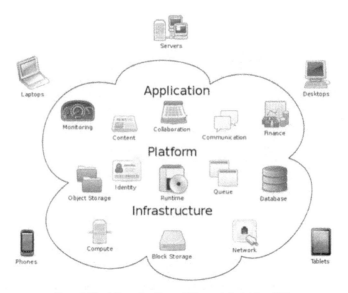

Figure 7: Cloud Computing Concept Diagram (adapted from [48])

As stated earlier and depicted in Figure 1, *Desktop grid computing*, the focus of this thesis, can be considered as computing on specialized grids in which processing cycles are used from desktop computers [80]. The cost of desktop grid is distributed over volunteers as each supports the expenditures for his or her resources (e.g. processors, memory, and communication bandwidth). The desktop grids are ideal for independent tasks requiring high computation. A central node is responsible to distribute the tasks and collect results. Desktop grid systems have progressed in two major directions; enterprise-wide desktop grid, usually called as *desktop grid*, and *volunteer computing* [115]. In the former, a grid infrastructure is restricted to an organization's boundary; spare resources of the organization's desktop PCs are used to execute internal computationally-intensive applications. Users have to comply with organizational policies so there is no point of volunteering resources. On the other hand, volunteer computing has emerged as a paradigm in which people and organizations connected through internet willingly share their idle processing resources for external compute-intensive projects.

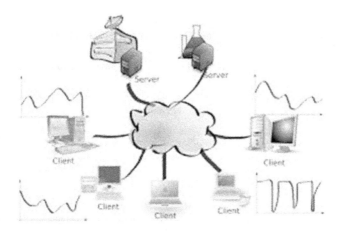

Figure 8: Desktop Grid Computing Concept Diagram (adapted from [53])

These two kinds of desktop grid systems are designed to tackle different applications. Desktop grids applications carry a small number of tasks compared to volunteer computing projects. The goal to be achieved through desktop grids is application's fast turnaround time, whereas volunteer computing projects seek high throughput, i.e., the number of tasks carried out per time unit. Figure 8 shows a desktop grid environment having different client availability.

Desktop grid systems have the capability to achieve the performance comparable to supercomputing. But, the reliability of desktop grids is low due to CPU and host unavailability. On the other hand, cloud computing enjoys the highest reliability due to specialized resources and core competency of the service provider. Cost of desktop grid system is on lower side as the processing is either done by volunteer processing nodes or by the nodes that are already available on the infrastructure. Grid computing is the most expensive compared to other variants of distributed computing due to the huge investment on a infrastructure that may contain many clusters.

2.1.1. Scheduling in Distributed Computing

Distributed computing paradigms like clusters, cloud and various forms of grids are likely to be the future of distributed computing. They have opened up new horizons for the solution of large-scale problems in various fields. Grids may have computing resources that are geographically dispersed and belong to multiple domains where each domain has its own access and security policies. These constraints cause resources scheduling, task scheduling and load balancing issues. Scheduling on a single processor system aims to fully exploit the CPU of the given machine, i.e., making the CPU busy all the time. In distributed computing, multiples tasks are created of a given application; these tasks are allocated to various processing nodes to achieve better turnaround time through parallel execution. Hence, scheduling in distributed computing consists of two main objectives [105]: a) selection of appropriate computing nodes to allocate given task, and b) the execution of various tasks of different applications on a particular computing node.

Scheduler is responsible to coordinate the execution of a given task on available computing nodes. When the scheduler receives tasks, its job is to allocate them on the appropriate computing nodes. This function of the scheduler is known as task allocation or task mapping in a DCS [95]. In a real scenario, multiple tasks can be submitted by different users, and the scheduler should be able to accommodate the stated multiplicity. The major aspects of scheduling are *turnaround time* and *throughput*. Turnaround time is the time elapsed from submission to the completion of a task;

scheduler's job is to minimize this time. Throughput measures the number of tasks successfully executed in unit time, and this needs to be maximized.

Reliability is also an important aspect of scheduling that can be defined as the probability of the successful execution of a task on the system. Task allocation made by scheduler should increase the reliability. Reliability is directly related to the throughput and turnaround time [109]. If the computing node is unable to execute the assigned task, then the throughput of the system will be decreased. This will also increase the turnaround time of the application that will make the system unreliable.

Fairness is another aspect of scheduling; in distributed computing, multiple processors are available and the goal is to obtain parallelism by distributing tasks among processors. Here fairness means that the tasks of various applications get equal allocation on the available processors [16].

When scheduler is playing the role of allocator, its first job is to analyze the concurrency present in the given job so that the job can be divided into various concurrent tasks. The second step is to allocate these tasks onto the appropriate processing nodes. Normally the task allocation mechanisms are designed to reduce or optimize the completion time. There are two ways to perform task allocation [91]. One is static allocation in which tasks once allocated reside on the same node. This requires prior knowledge including tasks sizes and service demands which is not available in most of the cases. Static allocation is easier to implement but cannot be applied in most of the real life scenarios. Dynamic allocation assumes that no prior knowledge is available and performs real time decision making. It is much more complex but achieves better throughput.

The scheduler can allocate single task as well as multiple tasks to the processing nodes. Single task allocation concentrates on one task and its completion. Multiple task allocation is much complex as the allocator has to keep track of the number of tasks from various applications and status of processing nodes on which these tasks are being, or have been, executed. To achieve load balancing, often the tasks are required to be migrated from one node to the other. This activity is known as task migration [117]. Load balancing and task migration are important characteristics to achieve reliability and optimize turnaround time.

Performance in a distributed computing environment can be referred to the average response time of tasks. The response time of a task is the time elapsed between its initiation and the first response it gets. The obvious way to achieve this goal is to increase the number of nodes in a distributed computing environment or to increase the resources on individual computing node. These solutions can be applied if and only if the existing nodes are overloaded. Overloading can be caused by uneven load distribution on the computing nodes across the system. Due to the random arrival of tasks and poor allocation methods, the system can go in a state where some nodes are completely idle and others are heavily loaded. Load redistribution or load balancing transfers the tasks from the heavily loaded nodes to the idle ones [117] to minimize the average response time. The main goal of load redistribution mechanism is to balance the workload across all the computing. To achieve this, one need to have some load assessment strategy that can estimate a node's workload on some measurable parameters such as hardware strength of computing node, total number of tasks assigned to a node, how demanding the tasks are in terms of computing resources etc.

2.2. Desktop Grid Systems

A desktop grid system is composed of a large number of computing and storage nodes connected through a network. These computational resources share their idle processing cycles and memory for the computation of large-scale problems. As the owner of the resources decides whether to volunteer or not, and give or not give the priority to the application running on them as compared to the one coming from the desktop grid system, the availability cannot be guaranteed for a definite period of time. The resources are also volatile due to user activity, hardware, software and network failures. Another factor that adds complexity is the heterogeneous nature of the computing nodes in terms of clock rate, memory and disk size, network connectivity, and other characteristics.

As stated earlier, desktop grid systems can be divided into two categories [115]. When the computers of an enterprise are used to increase the turnaround time of a compute intensive application, it is called *enterprise wide desktop grid* or simply *desktop grid*. The other category is *volunteer computing* in which home and enterprise computers take part by volunteering idle processing cycles to achieve high throughput. The design decisions for desktop grids and volunteer computers are almost the same, if the communication bandwidth issue isn't considered, most of the desktop grid frameworks works well for both. In this thesis, the term *desktop grid system* is used for addressing both the categories, i.e., enterprise wise desktop girds and volunteer computing.

The ideal desktop grid system should have four characteristics, i.e., *scalability*, *fault tolerance*, *security* and *manageability*. Scalability means that the system should be able to extend as and when required by adding more computing nodes and resources. The throughput should also increase proportionally with the increase in the number of resources. Fault tolerance refers to capability of the system to tolerate failures on server as well as client. Although traditionally, failure is referred to be software and hardware defects, for desktop grid system, in the thesis. this term is used to refer unavailability of computing nodes (host) as well as of CPU. Host unavailability is caused due to software, hardware and network failure whereas CPU unavailability is caused by keyboard / mouse activity that stops the desktop grid process. Security ensures that hardware, software and data must be protected from the desktop grid application. On the other hand, the desktop grid application components such as executable code, input and output should be protected from user intervention. Finally, manageability means that one needs to manage master and client end and expects the system to provide tools that can make the process easy and simple. The workers are expected to be non-technical users and they should be provided with simple client software that is easy to install and manage and can inform user about the statistics of shared resources.

Desktop grid system is based on client server architecture. Server's job is to take application from the user, decompose it into multiple tasks, send tasks to clients and collect the results, whereas the client job is to execute the assigned task and send the result to server. Here a procedural outline for the submission and execution of a desktop grid application is presented:

1. The user submits a job (an application) to the desktop grid server.

2. Server decomposes the job into smaller tasks (workunits).

3. Server looks at the available clients and selects the appropriate ones as per the job requirement.

4. Server assigns tasks to the clients.

5. Clients execute the tasks and send results back to master.

6. Master consolidates the results from all the clients and sends it back to the user that has submitted the job.

Most of the aforementioned steps are carried out by server, whereas only few are carried out on client. The responsibilities of the server are given below:

1. **User and Job Management:** The server's first job is to manage the users who would then submit the jobs. Server needs to host a database that can store the user and job information. Job may contain executable code comprising of the algorithm the user wants to run and the data that the code will use as input.

2. **Client Management:** The server should be able to maintain a list of available computing resources (clients) and should be able to store the related information such as CPU speed, available memory etc. This is only possible if a communication mechanism is available between the server and the client. This mechanism is also used by clients to download tasks from server and submit the results. In some scenarios the server should also be able to push tasks to the client.

3. **Tasks Management:** Server should be able to decompose the submitted job into smaller workunits / tasks. In some cases, this requires just chopping up large data files into small files. While in others, this may involve generating a lower and upper bound in the dataset so that the client can search the values in between these bounds. Identifying objects that the clients can evaluate is another possibility for decomposing jobs. When the server is through with this phase, the next is to allocate tasks to the appropriate clients. Client having the required computational power to complete the task within deadline are counted as appropriate.

4. **Results Verification and Validation:** Server needs to implement a mechanism to know about the submission of erroneous results from the clients. Server should have a mechanism to

validate the results submitted by various clients. The commonly used mechanism is to assign task to multiple clients and compare the results. Spot checking is another way in which a workunit is sent to the client for which the server knows the correct result. Server compares the results from the client with its own to check that the client returns the correct answer.

5. **Security:** Server is also supposed to implement some sort of security mechanism that can protects the client from "misbehaving" with executable code and vice versa.

6. **Performance Management:** Server should be responsible for the overall performance of the system and should be able to take necessary steps for the improvement. To achieve the above mentioned, server should keep track of the progress of individual task on the clients, overall job completion status that is based on the execution of individual tasks, client processing outcome and accuracy etc. Server needs to perform task migration incase the task has crossed the assigned / estimated deadline.

In contrast, the client software of desktop grid system projects has few responsibilities. The first is to collect hardware statistics from the client's machine and send it back to server (master). Then the client requests tasks from the server and in reply receives a set of filenames of the tasks to be downloaded from the server. Once the tasks are downloaded on the client, it starts to execute them one by one. This is done by running the executables on the given set of input file to get the output. The output is then sent to the server as a result. It is expected that the CPU of the client may become unavailable to the client itself. If this happens, then the task is not required to be restarted because of check pointing that save the state of process state after short intervals. The user on the client machines can set preferences on client software; importantly, how much RAM could be used by assigned tasks, how much idle time the machine should give to assigned tasks, how many files could be downloaded at a time and when a file could be downloaded.

2.2.2. Desktop Grid System Frameworks

The job of the desktop grid system framework is to simplify and automate various functions performed by server and client in a desktop grid system environment. As stated earlier, the desktop grid systems can be divided into desktop grids and volunteer computing. For desktop grids BOINC [6], OurGrid (peer-to-peer) [89] and XtremWeb [26] can be used. In case of volunteer computing, SZTAKI Desktop Grid [110] (for applications having less number of tasks) and BOINC (for applications having large number of tasks) are better choice. HT Condor [38] can be used equally for both.

Earlier, a general understanding of the responsibilities shared by client server architecture of a typical desktop grid environment is discussed. Based on the same, the desktop grid framework should be able to address the following queries:

1. How users submit jobs? Can a user submit more than one job at a time?
2. How tasks are generated from the given job? Will the tasks be dependent or independent?
3. How the granularity of the tasks is decided? Will the tasks be coarse or fine grained?
4. How clients register with server? What hardware parameters are polled from the client?
5. How the tasks are mapped on appropriate clients? How client's and task's preference matched?
6. How many tasks are given to a client at a given time? Can the number be changed?
7. How results are verified and validated?
8. How results from various clients are summed up to give user a consolidated result?
9. How fairness is maintained among various jobs while assigning their tasks to clients?
10. How fairness is achieved among the tasks of various jobs at client?

11. How fault tolerance is achieved as clients can become unavailable anytime?

12. How many replicas of a task are generated to achieve fault tolerance?

13. How many platforms are supported by client end?

14. How the client end users are kept motivated to donate processing cycles?

The above mentioned queries have a direct impact on application's turnaround time and throughput. These queries are mostly handled by the server end of the framework. All the desktop grid systems frameworks are capable of handling various jobs, multiple clients, pooling of client statistics and some sort of fault tolerance but most of them decompose job into independent tasks. Now, a brief discussion on some popular desktop grids framework is presented with a comparative evaluation.

2.2.2.1. BOINC

BOINC (Berkeley Open Infrastructure for Network Computing) is an open source platform developed at U.C. Berkeley in 2002 [2]. Today, approximately 60 projects are using BOINC in a wide range of scientific areas. BOINC server software is used to create volunteer computing projects. Each project has its own server and provides a web site. Volunteer connects to the website to download and install client software. The client software is available on Windows, Linux, and Mac OS X platforms.

A BOINC project can have more than one application [6]. BOINC provides flexibility for distributing data and intelligently matches requirements with resources. Having installed the BOINC client, volunteer can attach itself to any project. BOINC client can assign resources to each project. Attaching a project allows it to run arbitrary executables so it is the volunteer's job to assess project's authenticity and its scientific merit.

BOINC assigns a numerical value against the volunteer's contribution to a project. BOINC uses volunteer's email to perform cross-project user identification. BOINC client can also attach itself to a web service called an account manager rather than connecting directly to the client. The account manager passes client's credentials to sever to receive a list of projects with which client can connect to.

2.2.2.2. XtremWeb

XtremWeb is open source platform developed by INRIA [26]. Its successor XWHEP (XtremWeb- HEP) is currently developed at LAL CNRS. XtremeWeb is a lightweight Desktop Grid with some advance features such as permit multi-users, multi-applications and cross domains deployments. XtremWeb is designed in such a way that it can be used for desktop grids, volunteer computing and Peer to Peer distributed systems.

The XWHEP/ XtremWeb architecture consists of servers, clients and workers [119]. Server's job is to host centralized services such as scheduler and result collector. Clients work at user end; users submit applications to the server for processing. The client allows users to manage the platform and interact with the infrastructure as and when required such as job submission, result retrieval etc. Server schedules the jobs submitted by client on workers. Workers are installed at processing node to contribute their computing resources that are aggregated in an XWHEP/ XtremWeb infrastructure.

XWHEP improves the security of XtremWeb by the implementation of user accounts and access rights. These features extend user interactions over the platform that includes secure resource usage and application deployment.

2.2.2.3. OurGrid

OurGrid is an open source middleware designed for peer-to-peer computational grids [89]. OurGrid enables the use of idle computing and storage resources over a grid. These resources are shared in such a way that who has contributed the most, will get the most required. OurGrid provides a secure platform for the execution of parallel applications having independent tasks also called Bag-of-Tasks (BoT) applications. BoT examples may include parameter sweep simulations, rendering of images and many others.

In OurGrid, each grid site corresponds to a peer in the system. The problem of free riders (people who are not contributing their resources but using resources of others) is resolved in OurGrid by using Network of Favours mechanism. This credit mechanism ensures that the computing node sharing its resources will be prioritized over a node that is not sharing the resources. OurGrid Community, a free-to-join cooperative grid is also maintained by OurGrid team.

2.2.2.4. HT Condor

HT Condor (referred as Condor till 2012) is developed at the University of Wisconsin-Madison to provide high-throughput distributed batch computing [38]. High throughput computing refers to the efficient utilization of available computing resources to provide fault tolerant computational power. Condor is not only capable of managing dedicated resources such as clusters but it can also effectively harness idle processing cycle of any processing available on the infrastructure. Condor can process a task on an idle node. It is also capable of stopping the execution of a running task, marking a checkpoint and migrating the task to a different processing node. Condor can redirect the task's I/O requests back to the actual machine from where the task is submitted. As a result, Condor can seamlessly combine all the computing power of an organization.

Condor architecture is comprised of a single machine serving as the central manager and other machines that are part of the infrastructure. Condor's job is to assign tasks to the available resources. Condor client programs send periodic updates to the central manager so that the manager can be updated about the status of the resources and can make appropriate task assignments.

Condor uses ClassAd mechanism for resource matching. Through jobs assignment, the user can express job requirements as well as job preferences. Similarly, processing node can also state which type of job they are willing to run. Condor can adapt to any policy as per the requirements of the jobs and computing nodes. Multiple Condor installations can also work together.

Apart from framework like BOINC that are free for use, there are other proprietary frameworks designed for the same. Organizations such as Distributed.net [20], United Devices [19] and Entropia [11, 23] have produced proprietary frameworks (not available for free) for particular industries that can perform specialized tasks, such as searching for new drugs at pharmaceutical companies. Bayanihan [102] is another open source framework developed at MIT and is considered as the first web-based desktop grid system framework.

Many volunteer computing and desktop grid projects are using the aforementioned frameworks. Some well known volunteer computing projects are given below:

- Compute Against Cancer [14] helps researchers learning the arrangement and performance of cancer cells and make improved ways to monitor novel cancer drugs.
- FightAIDS@Home [27] models the progress of HIV drug resistance and assesses potential candidates for HIV drug detection. The project recently joined World Community grid, which now has additional than one million volunteers signed up.
- Folding@Home [87] learns protein folding, aggregation, misfolding, and associated diseases. It is managed by Stanford University.
- SETI@Home [104] investigates for intelligent living exterior to Earth. It is managed from the University of California-Berkeley.

Some popular desktop grid applications available at [71] are:

- Multiscale Image and Video Processing [MultiscaleIVideoP] is a BOINC based application that is designed to observe the dynamic behavior of material under mechanical deformation in loading machine by recording its evolution.

- Molecular docking simulations using AutoDock [AutoDock] is designed to predict how small molecules behave when they encounter a receptor with known 3D structure. It is available on XtremWeb, BOINC and OurGrid.

- City Population Dynamics and Sustainable Growth [CPDynSG] is a BOINC based data mining and statistical processing application that has the capability to investigate vast volume of data to perform predictions that can help in planning predictable population distribution.

- Patient Readmission Application [PR] is designed to rate hospitals on the basis of the level of readmission they get.

2.2.3. Design Issues in Desktop Grid Systems

There are many design issues in desktop grid systems but here only those issues are discussed that are relevant to this work.

2.2.3.1. Scheduling

The overall performance of desktop grid systems is dependent on effective scheduling which is the process of deciding how to commit resources between varieties of possible tasks. Due to the volatility of the computing nodes, scheduling becomes an important issue in desktop grid systems. Different scheduling policies are implemented in a typical desktop grid system that can be broadly categorized into three categories. Firstly, a *server scheduling policy* takes care of tasks assignment to server and is based on clients and tasks preferences (for example, size of the job, speed of the host, particular operating system, amount of disk space etc). A scoring-based scheduling policy assigns values to individual parameters used to calculate the overall impact.

Secondly, a *client scheduling policy* is related to CPU scheduling of desktop grid application's tasks (works on top of the local operating system's scheduler) and addresses issues, such as; which task to be executed from the currently runnable tasks? Which task to be kept in memory from the list of preempted tasks? Finally, the *work fetch policy* determines when a client can ask for more work and how much work can a client ask for?

2.2.3.2. Fault Tolerance

Desktop grid systems are prone to the inaccuracy of results and there can be many causes. Clients can connect to any set of desktop grid projects where each project may have different hardware setting requirements which can lead to different forms of error. The repercussion of any fault in desktop grid system is the increase in turnaround time of the desktop grid's application. Due to unavailability of CPU or client, results are delayed and client can also submit erroneous results either intentionally or unintentionally. The first one is handled by replication while the other is handled through spot checking and voting mechanisms. The details of these mechanisms are:

Replication is to assign task to more than one host in anticipation of a node failure. As the computing nodes in desktop grid systems are volatile, their availability cannot be guaranteed, which may include CPU as well as host unavailability. If such behavior is encountered near the end of task execution, completion time of task can be increased with large magnitude [78]. Replication increases fault tolerance but excessive replication also causes wastage of precious processing cycles. Replication can be implemented in three variations [78]. In *reactive* replication, only the replicas of already delayed tasks are generated. *Proactive* replication creates task replica at the time of task assignment and *hybrid* replication uses both proactive and reactive replication as per need. Replication not only helps in avoiding application delay but it also enables result verification.

Spot-checking, [116] on the other hand, is developed to assess whether a computing node is a saboteur or not. In this technique, spotter job is assigned to clients and its correct result is known to server. Master compares the result returned by the client with its own to decide about client. If the result matches with master's result, then the client is non-saboteur; otherwise, it is saboteur. When a client is identified as saboteur, it is blacklisted and will not be considered by master for future assignments. Master can also opt to do backtracking, in which all the results submitted by the client are cancelled. Saboteurs can be blacklisted on the basis of IP addresses and other credentials. Spot-checking is normally done twice to overcome the fact that the client has accidentally submitted wrong result.

Voting is the basic approach for the result verification. As the replicas of tasks are assigned to more than one client, same result from majority of client is treated as correct. There are two primary voting methods: one is known as majority voting in which the result that has maximum occurrence is counted as correct and the other is known as m-first voting in which any result having first m occurrences is counted as correct [101].

3. Related Work

This chapter summarizes the published work in the area of scheduling, replication, resource allocation and predicting resource availability (through Predictive Analytics) in context of desktop grids in particular, and distributed computing in general. Published work is divided into two categories: 1) *traditional techniques*, and 2) *Predictive Analytics based techniques*. The first category discusses the papers that have proposed scheduling mechanism / algorithms based on computing strengths, behavior or makespan analysis of the host. These papers also deal with grouping similar hosts and propose improved replication methods. Papers that incorporate fault tolerance mechanisms are also made part of this category. By using experimental methodology, these papers suggest improved results in various context. However, they use only traditional problem solving techniques. The second category presents papers which have implemented some type of statistical, probabilistic or machine learning algorithms / mechanisms. These papers gather data from real desktop grid systems, or establish test beds to gather data, implement aforementioned techniques and present promising results. From the literature review, key performance parameters are identified for the evaluation of task scheduling and work fetch policies.

3.1. Traditional Techniques in Desktop Grid Scheduling

The algorithm proposed in [37] is used for computing the batches of medium-sized tasks and uses worker's reliability, availability and lifespan as decision factors. This algorithm is designed for low latency computing in which deadlines are in minutes and hours rather than in days or months. Heien et. al. performed simulations to analyze the measures, and tasks are assigned

- 38 -

to the workers whose communication and computation is guaranteed. It is concluded that task assignment based on worker's speed and previous history, is more effective as compared to task assignment based on workers speed. Moreover, in [83], two mechanisms are proposed that can improve task scheduling in volunteer computing environment. The first is RMAX which uses makespan prediction model to allocate tasks to volunteers. It can work with almost parallel applications even having a limited number of volunteer clients. The second mechanism is RMXMN which is the upgraded form of RMAX. It uses the makespan of available volunteer clients as well as the reallocation methods to increase the robustness while doing the task scheduling. The combined features of robustness and makespan prediction make this mechanism elegant.

Kondo et. al. presented a mechanism for reducing the application's turnaround in a typical volunteer computing environment in [78]. The mechanism uses many resource selection and task replication approaches. Resource selection is performed by using resource prioritization and resource exclusion. Resource prioritization was performed in three ways. In first, the resource queue is prioritized on clock rates whereas in second, the same is done but 10-minute wait period is incorporated for each resource before doing task assignment. In third, resources' past performance history is also considered. For resource exclusion, four heuristics were used which excludes hosts whose clock rate is below 1.5, 1, 0.5, and 0.25 times standard deviation. It is concluded that resource exclusion based on makespan prediction is more useful. Finally, impact of various task replication approaches were also evaluated in the paper.

Krawczyk et. al. proposed an economic allocation system in [82] which is based on an auction protocol. Use of this protocol is a reasonable choice, as it is scalable with good turnaround time in grid systems without a large utilization deficit. This paper discusses the use of an economic resource allocation model in which negotiation of resources is done via an economic mechanism. A currency is used as the medium of exchange independent of economic mechanism employed. The paper details the simulation of three types of resource allocation mechanisms. Two methods are traditional, i.e., "volunteer pooling" which is based on traditional methods, and "fair share" resource allocation which is policy-based resource allocation. The third method is an economy based resource allocation known as "Reverse First Priced Sealed Auction" (RFPSA) in which jobs are put up for tender, and the lowest bid wins. RFPSA gave better results as compared to the other two traditional resource allocation methods.

Choi et. al. proposed a scheduling mechanism MAAGSM for heterogeneous environment based on mobile agent technology in [13]. MAAGSM creates volunteer groups on the basis of volunteer properties and allows the deployment of different task scheduling strategies as per group requirements. Mobile Agent-based mechanism provides a server frees architecture to significantly work in a heterogeneous environment and effectively reduces the task assignment to volatile clients to reduce incorrect results. MAAGSM scheduler performs fault tolerance by efficient replication. Moreover, in [114], the author proposed few policies to facilitate computing in heterogeneous environment. In such mixed environment, where the unreliable volunteers perform computing, it is necessary to quantify the results. The best policy which can work in volunteer computing environment for minimizing the average completion time, is an optimal policy and the authors compared various policies to get the best / optimal one.

Toth et. al. investigated the effects of task retrieval policies in a volunteer computing environment in [113]. Simulations were performed on different clients having single-core and multi-core CPUs to identify the critical parameters of different task retrieval polices that include "buffer multiple", "buffer none", "buffer one", "download early" and "super optimal". The idea is to identify a balance between the wastage of CPU cycles (client starts to download new task after the completion of previous one) and delayed result / increased memory usage (client downloaded to many tasks but unable to provide results). It is concluded that with single-core CPU, buffer-none and download early task retrieval policies perform better as compared to others, whereas for multi core CPUs, none of the task retrieval policy was able to outperform others because multi-core CPUs consume less wall clock rate. Apart from task retrieval policies, other project parameters such as file size, download speed, completion time, checkpoint time and internet connectivity also have an impact on the overall performance.

In [17], Daniel et. al. have studied the limitation of volunteer computing (VC) platforms for extensively parallel applications. They have concluded that it is really important to achieve collective availability (group of resources continuously available for relatively long time period) to enable parallel applications and workflows on VC platforms. This paper proposed and evaluated predictive methods using real availability traces from SETI@home and showed guaranteed prediction for the availability of collections of volunteer resources. Moreover, in [79], the problem of host characterization for accurate simulation in VC environment is addressed. The authors presented the correlation of volatility between resources and detailed a number of implications of these findings by using application-level traces of four enterprise desktop grids with a wide range of user bases.

Schulz et. al. proposed a platform for effective Peer-to-Peer (P2P) computing environment in [103], which can handle the architecture of P2P grids and is also capable of load balancing. The platform has a fine data gathering solution which is based upon pure reusable data aggregation system. Moreover, in [70], a framework is proposed for cloud computing environment. Dedicated servers are used for computation of data as a private network in cloud. This framework can be utilized to reduce the cost of that network by optimizing the strategy to improve resource grouping. Grouping the right resources lowers computation time as well as resource requirements.

Khan et. al. proposed a group based fault tolerance mechanism by focusing on selection of appropriate available volunteers on the basis of their hardware strength in [73]. The selection is based on workers processors cycle and memory, spot checking and makespan history. Replication mechanism produces replicas by evaluating workers behavior. Thus, replicas are only generated where required, which saves precious processing cycles. Furthermore, [77] analyzed the turnaround time and throughput of individual work units as well as same for the set of work units in a volunteer computing environment. The authors categorized the workers into two classes: 1) conservative (home) workers and 2) extreme (office) workers; having different availability patterns and computing and communication characteristics. For simulation, five client groups were created having a mix of conservative and extreme workers. Simulation results show that by increasing the number of replicas, independent work unit, turnaround time per work unit, and set of completed work units drops exponentially. If timeout decreases, the number of replicas will increase which ultimately decreases computation power. It is concluded that replication and timeout improves system performance when resources are of heterogeneous nature. Moreover, in [3], CPU speed, RAM size, disk space, host availability and network throughput of volunteers are taken into account for scheduling in volunteer computing environment. For analysis, SETI@Home host pool is used, which uses BOINC middleware. BOINC client measures hardware characteristics of the worker along with its host availability and CPU availability. It is concluded that hardware resources may be evaluated in combination, e.g., disc space is useful only if appropriate network band width is available to access it. Similarly, processor speed is useful when substantial RAM is available. Furthermore, different venues of volunteers (home, school and work) show different levels of throughput.

Sarmenta proposed a credibility-based voting mechanism based on voting and spot-checking in [101]. Credibility indicates worker's behavior which affects the job's redundancy. Credibility is estimated using spot-checking mechanism. The key idea is to evaluate the credibility of results based on voting, which improves sabotage-tolerance in volunteer computing, but on the other hand it is unable to determine spot check rate. High spot checking rate will cause excessive checking, whereas low spot-checking rate fails to ensure high reliability. Also, in [116], the authors focus on minimization of computation time in a volunteer computing environment. Spot checking of volunteers to establish reliability is a necessity in a hostile environment. However, high spot-check rate also results in the wastage of volunteer's computation time. Authors have proposed an optimized credibility based spot checking technique that uses ENR-based job selection. Here, jobs bearing fewer numbers of results are selected first. The proposed techniques facilitate the project owner by allowing them to select appropriate spot-check rate for the mathematical expectation of time T, so that computation time could be minimized. It is concluded that optimal spot check rate and expected computation time are good estimate to minimize the computation time with 1% uncertainty.

The work done in [75] analyzed CPU scheduling, work fetch, work send and job completion estimation policies based on BONIC middle ware which allows a worker to set preferences regarding resources sharing for each project, such as limit on processor usage, connection interval, scheduling interval, buffering etc. CPU scheduling polices are responsible of execution of jobs from the pool of all runnable jobs. Work fetch polices manage how much work to fetch and from which project. Work send policy establishes which job should be sent against

- 43 -

the worker's request. Job completion estimation can be based either on completed tasks of that job, or on duration. Idleness of CPU, CPU wastage, share violation and monotony were used as performance metrics and simulations were performed on the variants of the above mentioned policies. In [81], the authors proposed a group based replication mechanism for volunteer computing environment. This assumes that hosts are greater than tasks and the number of attempts on specific host is independent of other attempts on the same host. The mechanism takes volunteer behavior and credibility into account for grouping; hence replication for these groups becomes less problematic.

Silaghi et. al. investigated the issue of data security on un-trusted hosts in volunteer computing environment in [107]. The security of data can be achieved in multiple ways. The first one is to do symmetric encryption. Before data is sent to the host, the server encrypts the data with symmetric master key, which is created by hashing the time stamp with input file. The host is unaware of hashing. For decrypting the task file at host, a public key token is used. Another way is to use information dispersal algorithm in which file F is broken into N number of fragments, signed by the server and sent to hosts. This results in better protection of data files but the use of encryption techniques will burden the system. In [76], the authors proposed SNOW, a shared network of work stations platform which enables the use of independent work station for distributed computing applications. If these work stations are interrupted by the owners in the middle of distributed application execution then replication of some or all parallel tasks are required. Authors stated that in such scenario, replicas are to be created and the number of replicas is dependent on the availability of the workstations. The paper has also presented two workload models for parallel jobs that help in improving the results.

Morrison et. al. proposed a framework "WebCom" for task scheduling decisions in distributed environments in [85]. Here, server can assign the task to the volunteer clients in two ways, i.e., either sequentially or as control instructions. WebCom can interface with different computation engines. Control instructions are used to communicate with the computation engine. These atomic instructions are based on message passing. If the client isn't there to execute, then these instructions can be queued. Both client and master are capable of establishing the connection with each other. The connection once established, represents the channel along which instructions will be transmitted. Results are gathered on different channels using alternative port. WebCom lacks scalability and load balancing issues. The work done in [15] discusses the issue of QoS provisioning in grid computing environments consisting of dedicated and volunteer resources. The paper proposed that QoS can be provided through SLAs by exploiting different available scheduling mechanisms in a coordinated way, and applying appropriate resource usage optimization techniques based on differentiated reservations, scheduling in advance techniques and integration of rescheduling techniques. The experiments were performed in a real grid test bed and the results show that the proposed framework effectively harnesses the specific capabilities of the underlying resources to provide every user with the desired QoS level, while, at the same time, optimizing the resources' usage.

Klejnowski et. al. proposed a novel agent's delegation approach in [74] that improves the behavior of self interested agents by introducing incentive based cooperation method. This method offers reputation based as well as replication based strategies. Decision Trees are used to implement the concepts but the results are problematic. To cater for this, a multi-agent based "Trusted Communities" approach is presented that improves the results of delegation based incentive approach. The work in [10] investigates the problem of scheduling, while being faced with uncertainties of the availability periods and proposes a variety of scheduling heuristics to improve scheduling results in challenging environment. Authors evaluated the heuristics by scheduling a set of jobs under the constraints of unavailability periods of resources and identified the conditions of obtaining optimal stability, i.e., the goal is to reduce the effect of disturbance by calculating the ratio between the maximum completion time and predicted completion time. The paper presented a set of global and local scheduling procedures and performed simulation by using the actual desktop grid traces to analyze the performance, stability and execution time. The results suggest that Longest Processing Time (LPT) algorithm when merged with GreedySlack algorithm (in which availabilities are sorted by non-decreasing end date of unavailability and intervals are shifted by advancing their unavailabilities) delivers the best performance in terms of efficiency and stability with a reasonable cost. When cost is an issue, First Fit Increasing (FFT - one of the most popular pin packing heuristic) when combined with DAslack algorithm (which is a dual approximation paradigm that schedules jobs within various horizons until the minimum one is reached by using binary search) or GreedySlack algorithm, is the fastest strategy with decent performance.

Reddy et. al. proposed a *Comprehensive Performance Tuning Framework (CPTF)* in [96] which initially schedules tasks to different resources, analyzes the mappings from tasks to resource, and uses the analysis to tune scheduling parameters with the aim to minimize the overall throughput (completion time) of the system. The framework is capable of employing various scheduling criteria, dynamically deciding to process the tasks locally by considering the network availability, monitoring post scheduling performance degradation and performing re-scheduling as and when required. Parameters considered are: CPU availability, heap memory availability, combined mean availability of these two parameters, job size, job type, available grid resources, past execution history. CPTF first decomposes jobs into tasks based on available amount of CPU and memory. This is done by finding the maximum task size that can be scheduled with these available resources. Then relevant parameters are selected, based on which scheduling can give the best performance, e.g., by comparing execution time and task size. Overall, the framework is capable of handling the fluctuation of resource availability, variation in communication bandwidth and frequency of job submission etc. Simulations are carried out by considering various workloads, job sizes etc., and showed promising results.

In [72], the authors discussed the concept of computational economy as an effective solution to address resource-allocation problems and stated that less reliable desktop PCs are often underutilized, regardless of their price, because they do not exhibit qualities required by typical scientific and business applications. This paper addressed the problem of addressing QoS requirements of users along with an intelligent distribution of resources and proposed a Highly Available Job Execution Service (HA-JES) that fosters the balanced resource consumption by dynamically virtualizing resources to meet QoS requirements from users. HA-JES has been implemented as an extension of OGSA and results show that HA-JES is beneficial in terms of resource utilization, market capacity, and market stability. For clients, HA-JES gives more choices in resource selection and for resource providers, more revenues are earned with otherwise wasted resources. The biggest advantage of HA-JES as compared to an ordinary resource broker is the employment of dynamic and transparent replication strategy. The degree of replication is determined by the price of resources, client's QoS requirement and client' willingness to pay. HA-JES offers two different replication strategies. In "replication-space-only" strategy, replica is generated simultaneously on multiple service providers, whereas in "replication-time-space", replica is only generated when the job has failed before completion.

Moreover, in [118], Xavier et. al. have studied the possible benefits of using replication during task scheduling with the objective to minimize the makespan. As the nodes' speed may vary and is unpredictable, the problem becomes more complex. The paper provided a theoretical study of a well-known scheduling algorithm WQRxx that makes use of replication and proved the approximation ratios for this algorithm in different scenarios. The paper also presented a simple interface that can add replication to any scheduling algorithm. Simulations were carried out to verify the possible benefits of adding replication to several well known non-replication algorithms and results showed ample performance improvement. Also, in [121], a scheduling algorithm based on resource attribute selection (RAS), is proposed. The algorithm assigns a test task to the node to determine its resource attributes and then selects the optimal node to execute a task according to its resource requirements. The scheduling decision also takes into account the task completion history of a node, if available. The paper not only provides a formal definition of the resource attributes, but also computes the fitness of the resource nodes that is used for decision making. The process of identifying the fitness of the node is simple. The test task is assigned to multiple nodes and when the execution time of the assigned task on a particular node becomes equal to the average execution of the assigned task on all nodes, it is taken as maximum. The proposed algorithm is integrated with various scheduling frameworks that include Sparrow, Falkon and Gearman. It is concluded that when RAS is combined with Gearman Scheduling frame, it gives significant improvement in resource selection and resource utilization, primarily because of the load balancing strategies implemented in Gearman Scheduling framework.

Moreover, in [12], authors have studied the problem of result certification in desktop grids. They identified that the current result certification and scheduling mechanisms are static and do not adapt to changing desktop grid environments. They proposed a group based result certification mechanism that classifies volunteers into four groups on the basis of availability, service time and credibility. The mechanism applies various scheduling and result certification algorithms on the basis of volunteer group properties. They have also tried to estimate the rate of spot checking and redundancy by considering the same majors and also produced taxonomy of the result certification mechanisms. The work done in [21] presents a holistic picture of the current state of volunteer computing paradigm and elaborates the research issues in this field. The paper focuses on improving the task allocation to reliable hosts by analyzing the state of the hosts in terms of computation strength and reliability. The authors have presented a list of static and dynamic parameters on the basis of which hosts are grouped into various categories that result in improved task scheduling. Various task retrieval policies and their impact on the overall performance are discussed.

Yang et. al. raised the issue of optimized global scheduling for all submitted jobs in [120], while having the bottleneck of network bandwidth in mind. They proposed a network bandwidth-aware job scheduling algorithm which monitors resource usage and statuses for grids, using the Ganglia toolkit to further improve information services provided by the Globus toolkit. The grid resource brokerage system discovers and evaluates grid resources. Submitted jobs can then be executed by appropriate grid resources, meeting their requirements. The paper presented a comparison of bandwidth aware job scheduler with network-only and speed-only task scheduler and proves that the bandwidth aware job scheduler improves job execution efficiency. While addressing the significance of volatility in VC environments, in [92], the authors investigated resource characterization in order to derive efficient factors of host availability and the utilization of these factor for better decision making by the job scheduler, which results in improved system's performance. The authors have proposed a Scoring Availability Model that uses the statistical analysis of host's factors from actual occurrence in the trace data set. The results suggested independent and dependent factors occur frequently.

The desktop grid system server can use various factors for job assignment to host depending on host and job diversity (for example, size of the job and speed of the host relative to an estimated statistical distribution, disk and memory requirements for the job to be completed, homogeneous redundancy and host error rate). A scoring-based scheduling policy uses a linear combination of these terms to select the best set of jobs that can be assigned to a given host. From the literature review, various performance evaluation parameter are identified such as i) resource availability ii) makespan evaluation iii) replication iv) resource capability v) sabotage tolerance vi) group based design. By using these parameter, performance evaluation of various task scheduling mechanisms is conducted which is summarized in Table 1 on page 78. None of these performance parameters are considered collectively for such evaluation in the literature.

3.1.1. Taxonomy of Literature Review

Before describing the taxonomy of the literature review, performance parameters used in developing the taxonomy are brief described below:

3.1.1.1. Resource Availability

Availability of host is a critical factor for scheduling in a desktop grid system. As hosts are not managed centrally, they can become unavailable at any time. Scheduling mechanism must check host availability before assigning a task to any host. Host unavailability refers to the hosts being powered off, whereas CPU unavailability refers to a situation where host is connected to the server but its CPU is busy in performing host's local tasks. The configuration of desktop grid client is done in such a way that the host's CPU is only available to desktop grid when its not executing any local task, i.e., when the CPU is idle.

3.1.1.2. Makespan Evaluation

Makespan is a life time of a task during its execution from start to finish. The job of any scheduling mechanism is to minimize the makespan by assigning tasks to the better hosts. Once a task is assigned to a host, its makespan is estimated and if the actual makespan of the task matches the estimated makespan then the task assignment to that particular host is justified. This can also be taken as the "on-time task completion" and the scheduling mechanism should assign tasks to the hosts having better "on-time task completion" history.

3.1.1.3. Replication

As the resources are not under centralized administrative domain, there is a chance that they may become unavailable at any point in time. The solution to this problem is replication in which a replica of the assigned task is assigned to some other host as well. Replication helps in countering volatility, but excessive replication also cause wastage of processing cycles.

3.1.1.4. Resource Capability

Consideration of host clock rate or memory size to exclude or prioritize hosts at the time of task scheduling is a common way of resource allocations. However, focusing only on resource capabilities and not considering availability and reliability may result in poor decision making. Resources with low capabilities may be more reliable and can be available for more time.

3.1.1.5. Sabotage Tolerance

There may be hosts in desktop grid systems that try to submit erroneous results. To identify the saboteurs, spot checking is performed in which master assigns a task to hosts whose result is already known to master. Hosts that do not give correct result are counted as saboteurs and should not be considered for task assignments. There is also a need to verify the results computed by these hosts. Voting is one of the mechanisms and has couple of variants. In majority voting, results from the majority of the hosts are considered as correct, whereas in n-first voting, results from the n hosts is considered as correct.

3.1.1.6. Group based Design

It has been observed that grouping similar host helps in scheduling while keeping the cost low. This also facilitates in establishing various replication strategies. The idea is not to make decision making for each host but to establish same policies for similar host arranged in a group. The parameters of assigning hosts to different groups may vary and may include availability, reliability, computing strength etc.

The taxonomy of the literature review based on the aforementioned parameters, is shown in Table 1. 'Y' means the parameter is available in the proposed solution, whereas "N" indicates that the particular parameter isn't considered in the paper. It is also quite clear that most of the published work is focused on one or two parameters. Most of the proposed scheduling mechanisms haven't incorporated fault tolerance mechanism such as replication. Though there are some exceptions, either the replication isn't optimized or there is no sabotage tolerance mechanism, such as spot checking. Even the scheduling parameters used in the published work aren't very knowledgeable that result in poor decision making. The proposed mechanism i.e., GFTSRM, incorporates more knowledgeable parameters that result in better fault tolerant scheduling. Group based design not only helps in scheduling, but also improves replication. Chapter 4 presents GFTSRM methodology and chapter 5 discusses the GFTSRM experimental setup and results.

Table 1: Performance Evaluation of Scheduling Mechanisms using Traditional Techniques

Key Performance Factors / Reference No.	Resource Availability	Makespan Evaluation	Replication	Resource Capability	Sabotage Tolerance	Group based Design
37	Y	Y	N	Y	N	Y
83	Y	Y	N	Y	N	N
78	Y	Y	Y	Y	N	N
82	N	N	N	N	N	N
13	Y	Y	Y	Y	N	Y
114	N	Y	N	N	N	Y
113	N	N	Y	Y	Y	N
17	Y	N	N	N	N	Y
79	Y	Y	Y	Y	N	N
103	Y	N	N	Y	N	N
70	N	Y	Y	Y	N	Y
73	Y	Y	Y	Y	N	Y
77	Y	N	Y	Y	N	Y
3	Y	Y	N	Y	N	N
101	N	Y	Y	N	Y	N
116	N	N	Y	N	Y	N
75	Y	N	N	Y	N	N
81	N	Y	Y	N	Y	Y
107	N	N	N	N	Y	N
76	Y	N	Y	Y	N	N
85	Y	Y	N	Y	N	N
15	Y	Y	Y	Y	N	N
74	Y	Y	Y	Y	Y	Y
10	Y	Y	N	Y	N	N
96	Y	Y	N	Y	N	N

Key Performance Factors / Reference No.	Resource Availability	Makespan Evaluation	Replication	Resource Capability	Sabotage Tolerance	Group based Design
72	Y	N	Y	N	N	N
118	N	Y	Y	N	N	N
121	Y	N	N	Y	N	N
12	Y	Y	N	N	Y	Y
21	N	N	N	Y	Y	Y
120	Y	N	N	Y	N	N
92	Y	Y	N	Y	N	N

4. Group based Fault Tolerant Scheduling and Replication Mechanism (GFTSRM)

One of the goals of this thesis work is to reduce the application's turnaround time in desktop grid systems. Following research questions (reiterated from Chapter 1) are answered in this chapter:

- What is the impact of combining computing ability, reliability and availability on the applications turnaround time in desktop grid systems?
- What is the impact of grouping similar volunteers on scheduling in desktop grid systems?
- What is the impact of grouping similar volunteers on replication in desktop grid systems?

To answer these questions, a scheduling mechanism that performs better than existing popular scheduling mechanism such as, FCFS and PRI-CR-Excl is required. The approach presented in this thesis is based on simulations because of the unavailability of required number of computers to analyze the affects of scheduling policy on application's turnaround time. Thus, data is collected from client computers that could be used to formulate the problem as well as drive the simulations for proposed solution. The details of the data collection requirements and methodology, simulation for the problem validation and simulations of the proposed mechanism and associated results are discussed in chapter 5.

The chapter describes the proposed scheduling and replication mechanism to reduce the application's turnaround time. It is obvious that a more informed task allocation mechanism can resolve the problem caused by hosts having weak CPU clock rate or availability. The FCFS scheduling does not take much informed decision and assigns tasks on the basis of host availability.

This results in the assignment of tasks to such hosts who are unable to send back the results in time, causing delays which increase the turnaround time. When the task is delayed, the server creates a replica and assigns it to some other host. This requires the task to be executed from scratch on the new host. An obvious result is delay and wastage of processing cycles as the task has already been executed on some host to an extent. This shows that apart from careful selection of host, the scheduling mechanism should also know how to optimize replication. If the hosts that exhibit some common features in terms of processing capabilities and behavior can be grouped, then relevant scheduling and replication mechanism can be enforced in order to reduce application turnaround time.

A group based scheduling mechanism is proposed that can also be referred as a classification system. The idea is to group the hosts on the basis of such criteria that can be used to achieve more knowledge about task allocation. Three predefined groups named platinum, gold and silver are used in this work. On the basis of certain thresholds, hosts are assigned to these groups. The three measures used to assign a given host to a group are given below:

- Collective Impact of CPU and RAM
- Spot Checking
- Task Completion History.

Collective Impact of CPU and RAM: The work units in a desktop grid environment are assigned to hosts on various basis. One way is to accept the host having computing capabilities above certain threshold, e.g., accepting hosts with more than 2.6 GHz clock rate or rejecting host with less than 512 MB RAM. The author submits that the rejection of host only on the basis of one parameter is not a reasonable idea and other parameters should also be used to accept or reject a host. None of the desktop grid system mechanisms calculate the collective impact of computing resources explicitly. This idea is also supported by [73] which concluded that hardware resources may be evaluated in combination, i.e., disc space is useful if appropriate network band width is available to access it, similarly processor speed is only useful when substantial RAM is available.

To analyze the impact of the CPU and RAM relationship, a mix of integer and floating point operations were executed in a loop for 60 seconds on 1.8, 2.0, 2.4, 2.8 and 3.0.GHz processors having different RAM sizes, i.e., 512 MB, 1 GB, 2 GB, 3 GB and 4GB CPU and calculated the number of operations performed in 60 seconds. It is analyzed that there is a negligible difference in the number of operations performed for five set of configurations, given below in Table 3.

Table 2: Set of Machine Configurations used in the Experiment

Set of configurations	No. of Integer and Floating Point Operations performed (in millions)
CPU 3.0 GHz with 512 MB RAM	9840
CPU 2.8 GHz with 1 GB RAM	9834
CPU 2.4 GHz with 2 GB RAM	9825
CPU 2.0 GHz with 3 GB RAM	9853.2
CPU 1.8 GHz with 4 GB RAM	9811.2

Thus, it is concluded that the RAM should be counted as a collective parameter with CPU. Now, numeric values are assigned to CPU and RAM so that these parameters can become part of overall scoring method used for scheduling. The simplest way is to assign the highest numeric value to the largest RAM size or maximum CPU speed. The justification for the assignment of numeric values can also be taken from the experiments given in Chapters 4 and 5 that depicted that the hosts with better CPU cycles achieve better turnaround time. Hence, the assigned numeric values display the correct picture with respect to application turnaround time as well. Table 4 depicts hosts grouping by using CPU and RAM parameters and the assignment of numeric values on the basis of their effectiveness in task execution which is deduced by the experiment explained above.

Table 3: Grouping the Hosts on Speed and RAM size and Assignment of Quantitative Values

CPU – Speed scoring scheme	Value	RAM – Size scoring scheme	Value
Less than or equal to 1.8 GHz	1	Less than or equal to 512 MB	1
Greater than 1.8 GHz and less than or equal to 2.2 GHz	2	Greater than 512 MB and less than or equal to 1 GB	2
Greater than 2.2 GHz and less than or equal to 2.6 GHz	3	Greater than 1 GBand less than or equal to 2 GB	3
Greater than 2.6 GHz and less than or equal to 3.0 GHz	4	Greater than 2 GB and less than or equal to 4 GB	4
Greater than 3.0 GHz	5	Greater than 4 GB	5

Spot Checking: This is a way to identify a host acting as saboteur. In spot checking, tasks whose result is already known to server is sent to host and after the submission of result by the host it is cross checked with server's own result. If result matches, the host is marked as non-saboteur otherwise it is marked as saboteur [25]. Erroneous result submission can be done intentionally or unintentionally. This measure is used to ensure that the task is only assigned to hosts that are expected to provide correct results. Majority of the desktop grid system mechanisms allow the project owner to run spot check and restrict saboteurs. This process of spot checking is cyclic.

Task completion History: Task completion history states the percentage of tasks completed by the host before deadline. The deadline is defined by the owner of the application [75]. It is a major factor to place the host in a more reliable group.

4.1. Group based Scheduling Mechanism

In the proposed group based scheduling mechanism, there are three groups platinum, gold and silver. On the basis of collective impact of CPU and RAM, spot check results and task completion history, hosts are assigned to these groups. When the host login, its "collective impact of CPU and RAM" is calculated. In this process, host's CPU clock rate and RAM size are gathered and on the basis of Table 4, numeric values are assigned. After assigning values, percentage of scored marks are calculated, e.g., if a host scores 4 marks for CPU and 3 marks for RAM, then the overall score will be 7 / 10 i.e. 70% marks. The percentage may vary in between 20% to 100%. The second step is to perform "spot checking" that can result in either 0 (fail) and 1 (pass). If failed thrice in spot checking, the hosts will be marked as saboteur in database. The third step is to evaluate the "task completion history" that can range in between 0% to 100%. The available percentages of both the measures are divided in three equal parts. Platinum group is assigned the highest whereas silver group is assigned the lowest range. Hosts are assigned to these groups on the basis of all three measures and respective ranking percentages that ensure the assignment of better hosts to platinum group, followed by gold and silver as shown in Table 5.

Table 4: Criteria for Grouping Hosts

Group Title	Collective Impact of CPU and RAM	Task Completion History	Spot Check Result
Platinum	> 74%	> 66%	1
Gold	> 47% & <= 74%	> 33% & <= 66%	1
Silver	> 20% & <= 47%	<= 33%	1

The overall assignment of host to groups is based on all three measures but task completion history is taken into account first, after that spot checking and lastly collective impact of CPU and RAM is considered. To the best of the author's knowledge, these parameters are never used in the similar fashion for grouping hosts to improve applications turnaround time in a distributed environment. As shown in Figure 15, when the volunteer logins, its Cumulative Impact of Resources are calculated and recorded in database. Then a spot check is performed in which a test job is assigned to the volunteer whose result is already known to the master. This step is performed to verify whether the volunteer is a trusted entity or not. Tasks are assigned to the volunteers who have passed the spot check. Volunteers perform tasks and send back the results on the basis of which their task completion history is maintained.

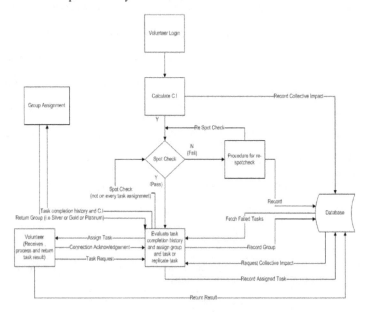

Figure 9: Group based Fault Tolerant Scheduling Mechanism

Initially, all the hosts are placed in silver group because of the unavailability of task completion history. As the application execution progresses, host's task completion history will change that will result in the update of groups (host will be moved from silver to gold or from silver to platinum groups) depending on the percentages of "collective impact of RAM and CPU" and "task completion history". For example, if the host scores >70% for collective impact and was able to complete 80% tasks assigned to it before the deadline, then the host will be placed in platinum group. If "task completion history" states a different group as compared to "collective impact of CPU and RAM", then the host is assigned to the group stated by task completion history, because task completion history is a more knowledgeable measure. A host with low hardware strength but continuous availability is always better than the host having high hardware strength and low availability. At the time of task assignments, platinum group members are given priority over gold group members. Silver group members are assigned tasks only if platinum and gold group members are not available.

Group assignment is a cyclic process and can also take place on worker's task request. For non-saboteur hosts, past history of task completion is evaluated and recorded in the database which will be utilized by the procedure that assigns individual hosts to a group. When the host sends back the result of assigned task within the deadline, the result is recorded in the database. This also updates the record of percentage of task completed on time for that particular host. Although the complete procedure is explained in detail, for more clarity given is the pseudo code for calculating the collective impact of CPU and RAM, spot checking and host assignment to groups:

Calculating the collective impact of CPU and RAM

(input loginid and sessionid)
    VarProcessorSpeed = Fetch_Processor_Speed()
    VarRAMSize = Fetch_RAM_Size().
    VarLoginId = Session (" loginID")
    Fetch marks for each component
    Calculate overallpercentage
    SaveInfoToDB(VarProcessorSpeed,VarRAMSize,VarLoginId).

Spot checking

(input loginid and sessionid)
    assign test job to the host
    VarNoOfSpotCheckFailed=0
    When host return result master will check whether the task is real or test task.
        If test task true
            Fetch masters own result of that test task
        If masterresult=hostresult
            SaveHostToDB "PASS"
        Else
            VarNoOfSpotCheckFailed = VarNoOfSpotCheckFailed +1
            If VarNoOfSpotCheckFailed=3
                SaveHostToDB "Fail"
        Else
PerformValidationforActualTask( )

Hosts assignment to groups

    VarPercentageCompleted, VarCollectiveImpact
    VarPercentageCompleted=getTaskCompletedPercent( )
    VarCollectiveImpact=getCollectiveImpact( )
    If VarPercentageCompleted >= 66% and VarCollectiveImpact >=74%
        Assign platinum group
    elseif VarPercentageCompleted > 33% & <= 66% and VarCollectiveImpact > 47% & <= 74%
        Assign gold group
    Elseif VarPercentageCompleted <= 33% and VarCollectiveImpact > 20% & <= 47%
        Assign silver group
    Else
        Assign NO group
    MaintainHostReadyQueue(orderbygroup)

4.2. Group based Replication Mechanism

Now the proposed replication mechanism is presented. In large distributed systems, inaccuracy in results is inevitable, and errors can stalk from many sources. Several causes of error can be computational [78]. Hosts can connect to any set of desktop grid projects where each project may have different hardware setting requirements. This can cause erroneous result submission [24]. The volatile behavior or slowness of volunteer resources near the ending of the computation can lengthen task completion period [13]. These problems have only one solution, i.e., *replication,* which means that a replica of the assigned task is to be generated and executed at some other host as well. But replication has its disadvantages. It uses processing cycles and excessive replication causes wastage of precious processing cycles. The replication can be implemented by 3 approaches i.e. proactive, reactive and hybrid [78].

In reactive replication, only the replica of delayed or failed tasks is generated. Proactive replication generates the replica at the time of task assignment for every task. Hybrid replication is a merger of proactive and reactive replication. By focusing on the grouping mechanism, replication is optimized. As the platinum group members are the most reliable, Reactive replication is performed for platinum group members. Proactive replication is performed for silver group member. Pseudo code of the replication mechanism used by silver and platinum groups is given below:

Host in Silver Group

Begin
*   do_ Proactive_Replication()*
*   For each task*
*   Create replica*
*   if task executed successfully*
*   show task execution successful:return_Result(param[ ])*

else if clone executed successfully

    show task execution successful by clone:return_ResultClone(param[ ])

    Increment task completion. history

    Loop for each Task

End

Host in Platinum Group

Begin

    do_ Reactive_Replication( )

    if task executed successfully

        show task execution successful:return_Result(param[ ])

    else create replica ( )

    if clone executed successfully

        show task execution successful by clone:return_ResultClone(param[ ])

    Increment task completion. history

    Loop for each Task

End

In hybrid approach, replication is performed when task has delaying risk, else no replica is required. It looks ideal that at task allocation, one can evaluate whether the task will execute successfully or not, but the question arises; how to evaluate which host requires replication or not? After considerable thought, hybrid approach is selected for the gold group in which "task completion history" is in between 33% and 66% as shown in Table 5. The same measure is used to answer the above mentioned question by cutting the task completion history range into half. The first half ranging from 33% to 49.5% represents a less trustworthy set of hosts, i.e., hosts closer to silver group, and hence, proactive replication will be performed. Reactive replication is performed when the task completion history is in the second half ranging from 49.5% and 66%, because these hosts are more trustworthy as they are closer to platinum group. Pseudo code of the replication procedure used by the gold group is given below:

Host in Gold Group

Begin

do_ Hybrid_Replication( )

    for each new task

    if host lies close to Silver Group(33%<= TaskCompletionHistory <49.5%)

        create replica

        send task to host

    else if host lies close to Platinum Group(49.5%<= TaskCompletionHistory <66%)

        send task to host

    endif

    loop through all new tasks

    for each submitted result

    if host lies close to Silver Group(33%<= TaskCompletionHistory <49.5%)

        if task completed successfully

            mark replica for abortion

            update user task completion history

        endif

    else if host lies close to Platinum Group(49.5%<= TaskCompletionHistory <66%)

        if task completed successfully

            if a replica exists

                mark replica for abortion

            endif

        update user task completion history

        else if there is a risk of delay or execution fails

            create replica if replica doesn't exist already

        endif

    endif

    loop through all results

End

This concludes the introduction of GFTSRM. In the coming section, simulations are performed using GFTSRM and results of GFTSRM are compares with the other existing mechanisms.

5. GFTSRM Experimental Methodology and Results

In this chapter, GFTSRM experimental methodology is explained that includes data collection requirements, data collection program, details of simulation to validate the problem simulation, several other details of proposed mechanism and the results.

5.1. Data Collection Requirements

Requirement 1: The data should accurately reflect the computers that might be available in any desktop grid system and should be significant enough to make some reasonable observation.

Addressing Requirement 1: A typical desktop grid system environment has many different types of computers depicting varied behavior and computing resources. In this work, computers available on the infrastructure of an educational institution are used that can be categorized in three categories: faculty computers, staff computers and computers available in laboratory (lab). In [86], authors have collected data from faculty, staff and system programmers computers. It is felt that the usage patterns and computing resources of these categories might be significantly different. To investigate this, maximum computer from each category available on the infrastructure were used. Specifically, 30 faculty computers, 10 staff computers and 50 laboratory computers were used. Other similar studies have used 68 university computers [113] and 11 computers [86].

Faculty Computers have different usage patterns as faculty members take classes on different days and timings in a week. These computers have an average processing speed of 2.84 GHz and RAM size of 3 GB. Staff Computers show similar usage pattern. These computers have an average processing speed of 2.02 GHz and RAM size of 2.1 GB. The usage pattern of laboratory computers peaks when a class is in progress otherwise it is modest. These computers have an average processing speed of 3.2 GHz and RAM size of 3.4 GB.

It is noticeable that computers belonging to different categories give varied availability intervals. Faculty computers' availability are normally for a period of 3 hours a day (when they are away to take classes), while staff computers are available for short burst of time because staff members are using computers throughout the day. Laboratory computers become almost unavailable during class commencement, otherwise they are mostly available. The average processing speed is not widely dispersed, i.e., in between 1.8 to 3.0 GHz.

Requirement 2: The data should reveal when the computers are available to participate; powered on but unavailable to participate refers to CPU unavailability, and when the computers are unavailable to participate refers to host unavailability.

Addressing Requirement 2: There are many ways to determine the availability of a computer system for participating in desktop grid system project. The simplest way is to identify when the user has given some input using keyboard or mouse. If the user has not given the input for a specified period of time, then it can be assumed that it is available. Operating system of the machine can provide this information. Another way is to analyze the CPU utilization rate and assume the computer is available when the utilization drops below some threshold. Another way is to see whether the screensaver is running; if yes, then the machine is available. This is a standard way as it is followed by all the major projects and same method is used in this work .

Requirement 3: The data should give insight about the affects of slow hosts having weak CPU clock rate.

Addressing Requirement 3: The simplest and effective way to determine the affects of slow hosts is by running a CPU intensive application for a continuous period on all the computers and analyzing the application's turnaround time. To satisfy the requirements 2 and 3, datasets used earlier are analyzed. Data set presented in [1, 81, 86] is not usable for us because none of them has defined unavailability in a way that can help in distinguishing between host and CPU unavailability which is required for this work. Although the data recorded in [113] distinguishes between host being "available", "unavailable but powered on" and "unavailable", they have categorized hosts in two categories, and the collection of data is also not continuous. Hence, the author has no choice but to collect data through experiments.

Requirement 4: The data should not be altered by data collection program.

Addressing Requirement 4: The data collection program needs to query operating system about the running of screensaver. It is ensured that the data collection program does not impose enough performance cost on the computer. A prototype of data collection program is executed on an old computer having 900 MHz processing speed and 250 MB RAM size running Windows XP. It is submitted that if the program remains unnoticeable on this machines, then it would be unnoticeable on any machine used in this work. The prototype queries operating system after every 60 seconds about the running of screensaver.

Through the task manager, the CPU utilization is monitored that remained on 0%. Query time is decreased to 30 seconds and then to 10 seconds but CPU utilization remained at 0%. So it is decided that a 10 second interval is used for the screensaver's start and stop. This is precise enough for the simulations carried in this work because a machine available to desktop grid system project even for 10 seconds can't go unnoticed.

Requirement 5: The data should be gathered for enough time to get accurate and reasonable usage patterns.

Addressing Requirement 5: It is obvious that the longer duration of data collection gives more accurate results, but it is not expected that such study would be able to find traces spanning over multiple months. It is noted that one of the study has used 28 days [113], the data collection in tis work also uses the same period, i.e., four weeks.

5.2. Data Collection Program

The design of the data collection program was dependent on several considerations, such as; how this program will be developed and for which operating system? How the program will collect and record data? The decision to select an operating system was dependent on two factors; first is the availability of operating system, i.e., operating system with a large enough pool of users and second is the minimization of development effort of this program. Obviously, it would be easier to write such program for a single operating system. Microsoft Windows operating systems satisfied both of the requirements. As the Windows operating system enjoys the lion's share of overall desktop operating system market, it is expected that the same will be predominantly used by the contributors of real desktop grid system projects.

After deciding Microsoft Windows operating systems as the target platform, it was time to think about the development of data collection program. Such program can be developed on Windows platform by using three ways, i.e., Windows Service, a Windows application, or a screensaver. As operating systems instruct the screensavers to start and stop, it is quite possible to create a screensaver that could log whether a user is idle on the basis of messages from operating system, but all the users are required to use the data collection program's screensaver to make the data collection possible. Since screensavers can be changed easily and users can intentionally or unintentionally change the screensaver during the experiment makes the screensaver an unfeasible option.

A Windows application running as foreground application can receive messages as a screensaver does to start and stop, but it requires some additional code. The application can be hooked with operating system to receive all keyboard and mouse events. In [98, 99] authors presented a dynamic link library (dll) to determine when the computer is idle for Windows operating system. However, this clearly incurs overhead that would alter the data to be gathered. Furthermore, Windows application is accessible through Windows Task Manager and user can accidentally or maliciously stop it.

Windows service does not require a user to log in to run and is not viewable through Windows Task Manager. Although the user can stop it, it is difficult for a user to know the actual working of the service which affects their decision to stop the service. Services can only communicate with the user through a log file, but as the communication with a user is not required in this experiment, this is not a problem. Windows Service can run on Windows XP which is the dominant version of Windows among the target user pool. It seems that Windows services can overcome most of the shortcomings of both screensavers and applications that make it a logical choice for the data collection program.

To analyze CPU and host unavailability, the data collection program records the data on hard disk, in case the computer participating in the experiment gets powered off by any means.

Recording the status of screensaver, every 10 seconds can use lots of disk space per day. "#" and "@" are written in the log file, where "#" represents that the screensaver was running and still is running, whereas "@" depicts that the screensaver was not running and still is not running. Whenever there is a change in the state of screensaver or incase of restart, time is written in the file. This will not only decrease the size of the log file, but also allow us to parse it conveniently. The service is designed on multi-threaded model so that when the computers are sending data to the server, they can continue data collection as well.

Whenever the screensaver starts on a computer, it represents the CPU availability and this is the time when the program that determines the affects of slow hosts on the application turnaround time is executed. It is required that this program is executed in a scenario close enough to a real desktop grid system in which desktop grid system application suspends/resumes due to computer owner's intervention. The program is designed as a compute-bound application that performs computation and writes computation rate periodically to a log file. For conducting the experiment, fixed length tasks are used and a mix of integer and floating point operations is performed in an infinite loop as done by Kondo et. al. in [78]. The 90 computers are kept fully loaded with the said CPU-bound requests. It is also noted in [78] that a dedicated 1.5GHz Pentium processor can perform 110.7 million such operations per second. Every 10 seconds, data collection program records how many integer and floating point operations have been executed and writes it to a log file.

It is decided that the computers running data collection program send the collected data to the server every 24 hours. Sending data directly to the server can create bottleneck on the server as computers participating in the experiment will be sending updates every 10 seconds. Although the chances of data sabotage intentionally or unintentionally by the user increases with the time data continues to stay at participating computer, as this work isn't overly concerned about sabotage, 24 hours timeframe is felt adequate.

The data collection program should run for a period that can ensure accuracy in the collected data and can give results quickly. The data should also be collected when the participating computers have ample load. The experiment was conducted for four weeks by the end of semester, as it is felt that this duration and timing of experiment meets all requirements.

After some preliminary test run, the data collection program on participating computers is executed in between March 01 to March 31 (2013). Traces are gathered from 50 laboratory computers, 10 staff computers and 40 faculty computers that showed the period when the computer was available for desktop grid system, unavailable for desktop grid system also known as CPU unavailability, and when the computer was powered off, referred as host unavailability. The traces also elaborated how many integer and floating point operations were performed by each computer that depicts the application's turnaround time.

It is found that the average of the total percentage of time computers were available for desktop grid system varied greatly, i.e., 31% for faculty computers, 45% for staff computers and 53% for laboratory computers. The average durations for the available, unavailable but powered on, and unavailable periods differed significantly in between the categories of computers. Laboratory computers showed least average duration for unavailable period which shows they remained powered on for most of experiment duration. Faculty computers gave the highest average duration for unavailable but powered on period which depicts that the screensaver didn't get much chance to run on these machines. Staff computers show the highest average duration for being available.

It was also observed that the staff computers gave the lengthiest traces because screensaver was changing state from start to stop quickly. This also depicts the short burst of availability from staff computers. Faculty and laboratory computer gave long burst of availability, hence their traces were short. It is found that the average availability interval of faculty computers remained below 41 minutes, whereas the largest interval was of approximately 5 hours. The average availability interval of staff computers was above 64 minutes in which the largest interval was less than 28 minutes. The average availability interval of laboratory computers was not more than 54 minutes in which the largest interval was of approximately 3 hours.

The closer inspection of the data on per computer basis with in a category also revealed different usage patterns. In particular, it is found that there were two laboratory computers that remained unavailable for most of the time during experiment which shows that they were not functioning. Similarly, few staff computers were almost never available for desktop grid system which shows that there was a continuous input from the users that has restricted the screensaver to run. These computers were used by the data entry operators. However, majority of computers were available for a substantial period of time to the desktop grid system.

With respect to the number of integer and floating point operations performed by each computer, the finding revealed that the staff computers having weak CPU cycles performed lowest number of integer and floating point operations. It was also observed that the among staff computers, computers having better CPU cycles gave better results, although almost all the computers gave equal short burst of CPU cycles. This suggests that the computers having weak CPU cycles were unable to complete the task in short bursts and caused delay in task completion.

5.3. Simulation for Problem Validation

In this study, an application consisting of independent and identical tasks is scheduled, whereas hosts are in order of magnitude of tasks. Hosts are individually managed by their users or owners and take part in desktop grid computation only when their CPU cycles are idle, due to which hosts availability is unpredictable. When a host becomes available to take part in desktop grid, it acknowledges the server through desktop grid software about its availability, and the server then assigns task to it. While executing a task, if hosts' CPU becomes unavailable, then the task which is in execution stops and resumes again when the host's CPU becomes available, whereas if host becomes unavailable during task execution, then the task will restart rather than resume. The most common scheduling policy is used which is known as First-Come-First-Serve (FCFS) in which server assigns tasks to the host that has acknowledged first. FCFS can be used with many desktop systems [6,26,38,89,110].

A discrete event simulator is developed that would use the gathered traces about the availability, CPU unavailability and host unavailability intervals as well as application's turnaround time using 90 computers. The study simulated three application having 450, 900 and 1800 tasks respectively. The selection of 450, 900, 1800 tasks is only due to get symmetric evaluation in the results. The parameters for the simulator are:

- **Task scheduling policy:** The method server use to schedule tasks to hosts, in this case, it is FCFS.

- **Task assignment time:** When the task is assigned to the host.

- **Expected turnaround time:** The time it takes to complete a task, if it is not interrupted. It is assumed that all tasks take the same amount of time, specified by this parameter, to complete.

- **Replication Start Point:** The time when the result is counted as delayed and replica of the task is assigned to some other hosts.

- **Download speed:** The client's download speed (in bps).

- **File size:** The size of the file required by each task that needed to be downloaded that include data file as well as executables (in MB).

The assumptions for the simulator are:

- File size is small (10 MB or less).

- Download speed is fast (300 kbps or faster)

- Tasks take 15 minutes to complete on a dedicated 2.0 GHz processor.

- When the CPU become available after some time, tasks will resume rather restart.

- The replication start point of a task is a multiple of 10 of the task completion time i.e. 150 minutes.

- Downloading a file takes fraction of CPU cycles cause of parallelism and its affect on the application's turnaround time is minimal.

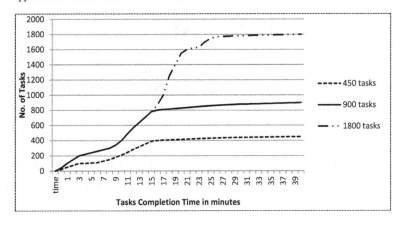

Figure 10: Turnaround Time of Three Applications having 450, 900 and 1800 Tasks

The simulation results depicted in Figure 16 indicate an initial edge after which application progresses approximately linearly. It is observed that in case of 450 tasks, 90% of tasks were completed in 21 minutes, whereas rest of the tasks took 41 minutes that means, last 10% of the tasks took almost equal time to complete as compared to initial 90% of the tasks. Same behavior was observed with application of 900 and 1800 tasks. It can be said that fast host have completed their assigned tasks due to which an initial edge was observed whereas slow hosts caused task failure due to which replication took place hence caused other hosts to perform tasks from beginning and ultimately resulted in application delay.

On the basis of above mentioned findings, It is hypothesized that hosts behaving slowly due to their clock rates, and hosts having variations in their availability, can cause task failure which ultimately results in application delay hence causes increases in application's turnaround time. It is noted in [37] that the delayed correct results and erroneous results may cause wastage of CPU cycles. Delayed correct results are normally received after extensive replication which itself causes wastage of CPU cycles.

5.4. Results of GFTSRM

Simulations are performed using the collected traces and with the same parameter and assumptions used for problem validation. However there are few differences as well. First, the effectiveness of the proposed mechanism as compared to other scheduling mechanisms is to be determined, that is why simulations are performed using three scheduling mechanism: FCFS, PRI-CR-Excl [1] and GFTSRM. FCFS schedules task on the first come first serve basis, whereas PRI-CR-Excl scheduling excludes hosts having clock rates below some defined clock rate threshold value. The intention is to evaluate how much improvement can be achieved through the proposed mechanism as compared to FCFS and PRI-CR-Excl. FCFS is chosen for the comparison with the proposed mechanism because it is used by most Desktop grid systems. In addition to FCFS, PRI-CR-Excl is used for comparison because of the claim that RAM should also be considered as parameter for such decision making.

The second difference in the simulation as compared to the one carried out for problem validation is that now applications varying in task size are used cause increase in task size, increases task failure in linear fashion, as concluded in [78]. Applications are used consisting 450, 900 and 1800 independent tasks for simulation. Furthermore each application has three instances consisting 5, 15 and 35 minutes of tasks respectively. Separate simulations are carried for varied number of tasks and task sizes using proposed mechanism, FCFS and PRI-CR-Excl. Available number of simulated hosts are 90. As stated earlier, the selection of 450, 900, 1800 tasks is only due to get symmetric evaluation in the results.

The problem definition suggested that hosts behaving slow due to their clock rates and hosts having variations in their availability can cause task failure which ultimately results in application delay and increased application's turnaround time. The aim of this work is to reduce the applications turnaround time in desktop grid environment, that's why tasks makespan is selected as the performance metrics. If the individual task's makespan is reduced than the overall application's turnaround time will automatically be optimized. The proposed mechanism is compared with FCFS and PRI-CR-Excl on the basis of the above mentioned performance metrics. The comparison is performed on step wise basis to analyze the impact of each step i.e. hosts selection based on collective impact of CPU and RAM without grouping, host selection based on grouping mechanism, impact of various task replication mechanism and impact of overall mechanism – group based scheduling and replication.

5.4.1. Results of Selecting Hosts based on Collective Impact of CPU and RAM

In this method, focus is on host's computing capability strength in terms of CPU and RAM. Both components are assigned a numeric value according to the ranges defined in Table 4, then aggregate of those assigned values are calculated. If a resource obtains 70% or higher marks, then it will be allowed to serve as desktop grid system client. Key idea behind the approach is to eliminate slow hosts which might cause task failure and application delay.

Simulations were performed to observe the difference between FCFS, PRI-CR-Excl and resource selection based on collective impact of CPU and RAM. Figure 17 shows makespan achieved for applications having 450, 900, 1800 tasks through FCFS, PRI-CR-Excl and collective impact. It is observed that the host selection based on collective impact shows better makespan as compared to FCFS and PRI-CR-Excl in all cases. The reasons are, FCFS must have selected slow hosts as it performs scheduling on first come first serve basis, whereas PRI-CR-Excl must have rejected hosts on the basis of low CPU speed. On the other hand, the collective impact would neither have chosen slow hosts nor have rejected hosts just on the basis of CPU because it considers RAM as well in decision making.

Furthermore, applications having tasks with length of 5 misnutes show least makespan than the applications having 15 or 35 minute length. The reason behind this is the granularity of tasks due to which even the host whose availability interval is short, can complete the task. In addition to this, 450 tasks are less than the available number of hosts which allow scheduler to assign tasks to hosts whose collective impact is relatively high.

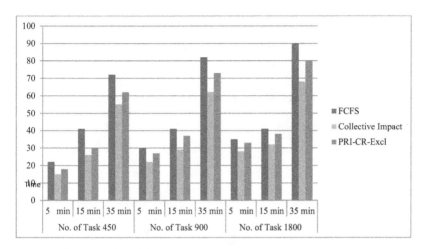

Figure 11: Applications Completion Time using FCFS, PRI-CR-Excl and Collective Impact of CPU and RAM

In case of 900 and 1800, tasks makespan is increased as compared to 450 tasks which shows that scheduler has assigned tasks to such hosts that were not considered in case of 450 tasks. As the number of tasks would increase scheduler will have to assign tasks to weak hosts.

In the coming section, the impact of overall grouping mechanism is presented that not only includes collective impact of CPU and RAM, but also spot checking and task completion history. Addition of these mechanisms have improved the results because these methods have eliminated the saboteurs (intentional or un-intentional) and have considered the host past performance.

5.4.2. Results of Selecting Hosts based on Grouping Mechanism

Here, the application turnaround time of FCFS, PRI-CR-Excl and GFTSRM based on collective impact of CPU and RAM, spot check and task completion history is examined. Comparison of Figure 17 and Figure 18 shows that the grouping mechanism not only outperforms the FCFS and PRI-CR-Excl, but also improves the results of collective impact of CPU and RAM (when used independently). Task assignment to slow host in FCFS must have caused task failure that has enforced scheduler to assign those tasks to other hosts for execution form the scratch. PRI-CR-Excl performed better than FCFS, but consumed little more time than proposed grouping mechanism. PRI-CR-Excl excludes resources which possess slow clock rate, but because of enhanced RAM size, may have completed the task. Due to this factor PRI-CR-Excl causes wastage of CPU cycles.

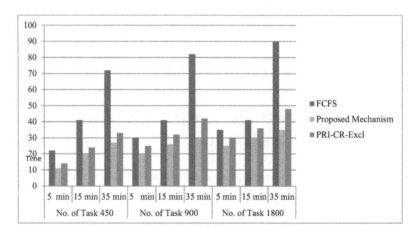

Figure 12: Applications Completion Time using FCFS, PRI-CR-Excl and Proposed Grouping Mechanism

The proposed grouping mechanism performed better because it provides a facility in which resource's internal processing capability is measured cumulatively due to which some slow clock rate hosts having higher RAM can join desktop grid which eliminates the aspect of CPU wastage, so by the utilization of such CPU cycles, proposed grouping mechanism improves application latency.

5.4.3. Results of Task Replication

Two measures are considered to evaluate the impact of replication; one is the wastage of CPU cycles and second is the application turnaround time. The reason for selecting these measures are simple; replication is performed to decrease the application turnaround time and if not done carefully, it can increase the wastage of CPU cycles that is why it is felt that the replication is closely related to stated measures.

Simulations are performed for the proactive and reactive replication without grouping mechanism. The application of 900 tasks is considered which is using 450 simulated hosts. The turnaround time of this application without replication is close to 42 minutes as depicted in Figure 1. Proactive replication is performed in which all the task assignments are replicated, i.e., each task is assigned to two hosts followed by a reactive replication in which replica is only generated when task fails. The results shown in Figure 19a, 19b suggest that proactive replication wastes more CPU cycles as compared to the reactive replication, whereas the turnaround time in reactive replication is greater than proactive replication. The reason proactive replication causes wastage of CPU cycles is that the reliable hosts executed the task successfully so replicating their task caused wastage of CPU cycles. Proactive replication is suitable when hosts are not reliable or tasks are allocated to known slow host.

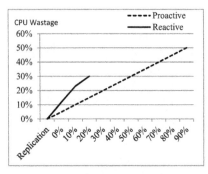
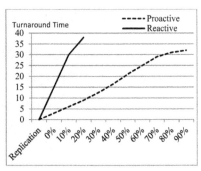

Figure 19a   Figure 19b

Figure 13: Proactive and Reactive Approaches of Replication without Grouping Mechanism

The reason of high turnaround time due to reactive replication is simple; the replicas are only generated when the failure or delay has already occurred. Reactive replication saves CPU cycles but delay in result submission causes increase in the applications turnaround time.

The balance between the two measures i.e. wastage of CPU cycles and application turnaround time can only be achieved, if the hosts having similar computing capabilities (CPU and RAM) and behaviors (reliability and task completion history) can be grouped together. The proposed grouping mechanism has already categorized hosts into platinum, gold and silver groups, now the question is which replication mechanism is best suited for a particular group. Platinum group possesses reliable clients in terms of computation capability and task completion history so platinum group does not require full replication due to which platinum group is assigned reactive replication. The hosts of the silver group are the least reliable one that is why proactive replication is used for silver group. Now proactive and reactive replication is performed on the basis of silver and platinum groups.

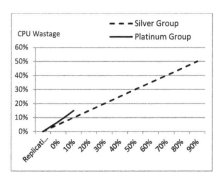
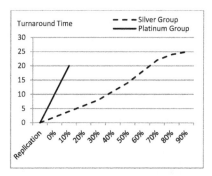

Figure 20a   Figure 20b

Figure 14: Proactive and Reactive Approaches of Replication with Grouping Mechanism

The results presented in Figure 20a show significant improvement in CPU wastage as compared to Figure 19a for reactive replication (used for platinum group), because this group consists of better hosts that rarely fail or delay the task. This reduces replication which causes CPU wastage. The CPU wastage of proactive replication (used for silver group) almost remained same because replicas were generated at the time of task assignment for each task allocated to the host of silver group. Figure 20b shows improvement in the application turnaround time as compared to Figure 19b for both type of replications i.e. proactive (used for silver group) and reactive (used for platinum group) because the replication mechanisms used for each group is suitable for the respective group members that improve the overall application turnaround time.

In hybrid approach, replication is performed when the task has delaying risk, else no replica is required. It looks ideal that at task allocation, one can evaluate whether the task will execute successfully or not, but the question arises; how to evaluate which host require replica or not? Hybrid approach is used for the gold group which uses the task completion history for answering the above mentioned question. If the task completion history is in between 33% to 49.5%, then the host is close to silver group, hence proactive replication will be performed. Reactive replication is performed when the task completion history is in between 49.5% and 66 because at this point the host is closer to platinum group. The results in Figure 21a, 21b show that a balance is kept in between CPU cycle wastage and application execution time i.e. both CPU wastage and Turnaround time lie in between platinum and silver groups.

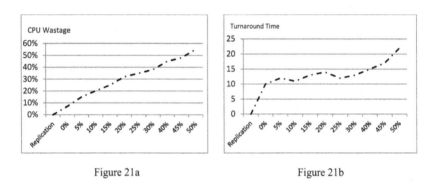

Figure 21a   Figure 21b

Figure 15: Gold group with Hybrid Approach of Replication

The combination of various replication mechanisms have resulted in the optimization of the overall mechanism because for each group, only that replication mechanism is used that can produce the optimized result.

5.4.4. Overall Result of GFTSRM

To analyze the overall impact, three applications (used for Figure 16) are used again, each having 450, 900 and 1800 tasks respectively. The task length was same in all the three application i.e. 15 minutes of length. Here 450 hosts are used but now the replication mechanism is appended to the group based resource scheduling mechanism.

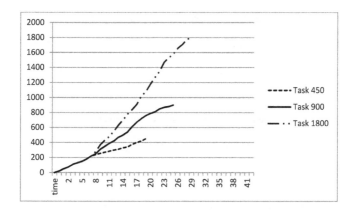

Figure 16: Turnaround Time of Applications using GFTSRM

The results depicted in Figure 22 shows that application with 450 tasks took 20 minutes, whereas the applications with 900 and 1800 tasks took 26 and 30 minutes to complete respectively. A comparison of figure 1 and 8 shows a significant improvement in application turnaround time, that is why it is safe to say that the arrangement of hosts into groups is as per their computational strength and task completion history, while each group has a relevant replication policy which can reduce the application turnaround time.

5.4.5. Validation of Simulation Results

In order to validate the GFTSRM simulation results, an experiment was conducted using GFTSRM on the same 90 computers that were used for generating the traces for all the simulations. Three applications consisting of 45, 90 and 180 respectively were used, the reason for choosing the given number of tasks is to achieve symmetric evaluation of results when tasks are half, equal and double than available number of hosts.

It is observed that 45 tasks took almost 2.8 minutes to complete, whereas 90 and 180 tasks took 3.2 and 3.5 minutes respectively. The validation results do not portray the exact picture created by the simulations given in figure 8, but still these results are acceptable as the overall difference in application's turnaround time is less than 12.5%. This also shows that the assumptions taken into account for simulations such as bandwidth, task download impact on CPU utilization had more impact on processing than expected.

Hence, the research question presented in chapter 1 and 4 can be answered as follows:

- GFTSRM used computing ability (collective impact of processing cycles and memory), reliability (spot checking) and availability (makespan statistics) for group based scheduling that resulted in the reduction of applications turnaround time in desktop grid systems.

- GFTSRM grouped similar hosts in three groups, i.e., platinum, gold and silver. Platinum hosts the most reliable hosts whereas silver hosts the unreliable ones. Gold carries hosts that reliable but may delay the tasks. GFTSRM performed well as compared to FCFS and PRI-CR-Excl that proves grouping similar volunteers improves scheduling in desktop grid systems.

- GFTSRM improved the replication in desktop grid system by identifying relevant replication mechanism for each group. GFTSRM used reactive replication (replica is generated when the task has been delayed) for platinum group and proactive replication (replica is generated at the time of actual task assignment) for silver group. The gold group used hybrid replication mechanism which is a merger of proactive and reactive replication.

6. Conclusion

Desktop grid systems are effective and attractive platforms for executing large computations, because they offer a high return on investment by using the idle capacity of an existing computing infrastructure. This thesis has focused on the issue of task scheduling / resource allocation process in desktop grid systems and presented several concrete contributions:

The thesis analyzed various task scheduling mechanism used by the server and different work fetch and CPU scheduling mechanisms used by the clients. An application is developed to understand the correlation between the RAM size and CPU clock rate on the processing time. On the basis of the findings, a host selection mechanism based on the collective impact of processing cycles and memory is proposed that was not done earlier by any desktop grid system mechanism.

A Group based Fault Tolerant Scheduling and Replication Mechanism (GFTSRM) is proposed that group hosts on the basis of spot checking, makespan statistics and collective impact of processing cycles and memory. Three groups are proposed i.e. platinum, gold and silver. Platinum hosts the most reliable hosts whereas silver hosts the unreliable ones. Gold carries hosts that are not unreliable but may delay the tasks.

Relevant replication mechanisms are identified for each group. Reactive replication (replica is generated when the task has been delayed) is performed for platinum group and proactive replication (replica is generated at the time of actual task assignment) for silver group. The gold group uses hybrid replication mechanism which is a merger of proactive and reactive replication.

The actual data of 90 computers having different resource capabilities and behavior is used to compare GFTSRM with FCFS and PRI-CR-Excl scheduling mechanisms. The results of GFTSRM are compared with FCFS because FCFS simply schedules jobs on first come first server basis and used by most volunteer computing system in recent time [78]. In addition to FCFS, PRI-CR-Excl [78] is also used for comparison purpose which excludes hosts on the basis of fixed clock rates. PRI-CR-Excl is used for comparison because GFTSRM excludes hosts on the basis of "collective impact of CPU and RAM".

It is shown that the appropriate scheduling and replication mechanisms can only be implemented after the grouping of resources on computing strength and behavior. Simulation and validation results have also confirmed that the GFTSRM allocated tasks to hosts with higher probability of tasks completion that resulted in the minimization of tasks failures, improvement in fault tolerance and reduction of application's turnaround time of desktop grid system projects.

7. Future Work

There are a number of ways in which this work can be extended:

1.   The proposed mechanism is expected to be effective in internet environments but neither the traces are taken from Internet based desktop grids nor it is evaluated via simulation. The effectiveness of the proposed mechanism cannot be ascertained for Internet environments. It is suggested that the traces from internet environment would facilitate to prove the effectiveness in the said environment.

2.   In this work, applications consisting of independent tasks are used that have simplified the problem. It would be interesting to use the proposed mechanism with applications having task dependencies.

3.   The proposed scheduling mechanism cannot maintain fairness among the tasks of multiple applications, while assigning resources. This is a requirement for a real world scenario and a possible extension of this work.

4.   Although various work fetch mechanisms are studied in this work, their effectiveness for the proposed mechanism isn't evaluated. This work can be extended to find the work fetch mechanism that suits best for the proposed scheduling mechanism.

8. References

1. Acharya, A., Edjlali, G., Saltz, J. (1997). The utility of exploiting idle workstations for parallel computation. In Proceedings of SIGMETRICS'97, pp. 225–234. Seattle, Washington, USA

2. Anderson, D. P. (2004, November). Boinc: A system for public-resource computing and storage. In Grid Computing, 2004. Proceedings. Fifth IEEE/ACM International Workshop on (pp. 4-10). IEEE.

3. Anderson, D. P., & Fedak, G. (2006, May). The computational and storage potential of volunteer computing. In Cluster Computing and the Grid, 2006. CCGRID 06. Sixth IEEE International Symposium on (Vol. 1, pp. 73-80). IEEE.

4. Anjos, J. C., Carrera, I., Kolberg, W., Tibola, A. L., Arantes, L. B., & Geyer, C. R. (2015). MRA++: Scheduling and data placement on MapReduce for heterogeneous environments. Future Generation Computer Systems, 42, 22-35.

5. Barnatt, C. (2010). A Brief Guide to Cloud Computing: An essential guide to the next computing revolution. Hachette UK.

6. Berkeley Open Infrastructure for Network Computing accessible from http://boinc.berkeley.edu/

7. Brevik, J., Nurmi, D., & Wolski, R. (2004, April). Automatic methods for predicting machine availability in desktop grid and peer-to-peer systems. In Cluster Computing and the Grid, 2004. CCGrid 2004. IEEE International Symposium on (pp. 190-199). IEEE.

8. Camiel, N., London, S., Nisan, N., & Regev, O. (1997, April). The popcorn project: Distributed computation over the internet in java. In 6th International World Wide Web Conference.

9. Camm J., Cochran J., Fry M. J., Ohlmann J., Anderson D., (2014), Essential of Business Analytics, Cengage Learning.

10. Canon, L. C., Essafi, A., & Trystram, D. (2014). A Proactive Approach for Coping with Uncertain Resource Availabilities on Desktop Grids. FEMTO-ST, Tech. Rep. RRDISC2014-1.

11. Chien, A., Calder, B., Elbert, S., & Bhatia, K. (2003). Entropia: architecture and performance of an enterprise desktop grid system. Journal of Parallel and Distributed Computing, 63(5), 597-610.

12. Choi, S., & Buyya, R. (2010). Group-based adaptive result certification mechanism in Desktop Grids. Future Generation Computer Systems, 26(5), 776-786.

13. Choi, S., Baik, M., Gil, J., Jung, S., & Hwang, C. (2006). Adaptive group scheduling mechanism using mobile agents in peer-to-peer grid computing environment. Applied Intelligence, 25(2), 199-221.

14. Compute Against Cancer Project accessible from http://www.computeagainstcancer.org/

15. Conejero, J., Caminero, B., Carrión, C., & Tomás, L. (2014). From volunteer to trustable computing: Providing QoS-aware scheduling mechanisms for multi-grid computing environments. Future Generation Computer Systems,34, 76-93.

16. Coulouris, G., Dollimore, J., & Kindberg, T. (1994). Distributed Systems Concepts and Design, Addison Wesley.

17. Daniel Lazaro, Derrick Kondo and Joan Manuel Marques, "Long-term availability prediction for groups of volunteer resources," Journal of Parallel Distributed Computing 72 (2012) 281–296

18. Data Synapse Inc. accessible from http://www.datasynapse.com/

19. Derrick, Harris, (2007), "The Evolution of United Devices (and Grid, In General)", Grid Today.

20. Distributed.Net, accessed from http://www.distributed.net

21. Durrani, M. N., & Shamsi, J. A. (2014). Volunteer computing: requirements, challenges, and solutions. Journal of Network and Computer Applications,39, 369-380.

22. Einstein Physics and Astronomy Project accessible from http://einstein.phys.uwm.edu/

23. Entropia, Inc. accessible from http://www.entropia.com

24. Estrada, T., Fuentes, O., & Taufer, M. (2008). A distributed evolutionary method to design scheduling policies for volunteer computing. ACM SIGMETRICS Performance Evaluation Review, 36(3), 40-49.

25. Estrada, T., Taufer, M., & Reed, K. (2009, May). Modeling job lifespan delays in volunteer computing projects. In Proceedings of the 2009 9th IEEE/ACM International Symposium on Cluster Computing and the Grid (pp. 331-338). IEEE Computer Society

26. Fedak, G., Germain, C., Neri, V., & Cappello, F. (2001). Xtremweb: A generic global computing system. In Cluster Computing and the Grid, 2001. Proceedings. First IEEE/ACM International Symposium on (pp. 582-587). IEEE.

27. Fight Aids Project accessible from http://www.fightaidsathome.org/

28. Finger, M., Bezerra, G. C., & Conde, D. R. (2010). Resource use pattern analysis for predicting resource availability in opportunistic grids. Concurrency and Computation: Practice and Experience, 22(3), 295-313.

29. Foster, I., & Kesselman, C. (2003). What is the Grid. A three point checklist, Grid Today (1), 343-354.

30. Gao, L., & Malewicz, G. (2007). Toward maximizing the quality of results of dependent tasks computed unreliably. Theory of Computing Systems, 41(4), 731-752.

31. Ghormley, D. P., Petrou, D., Rodrigues, S. H., Vahdat, A. M., & Anderson, T. E. (1998). GLUnix: A Global Layer Unix for a network of workstations.Software Practice and Experience, 28(9), 929-961

32. Gil, J. M., & Jeong, Y. S. (2014). Task scheduling scheme by checkpoint sharing and task duplication in P2P-based desktop grids. Journal of Central South University, 21(10), 3864-3872.

33. Gil, J. M., Kim, S., & Lee, J. (2013). Task Replication and Scheduling Based on Nearest Neighbor Classification in Desktop Grids. In Ubiquitous Information Technologies and Applications (pp. 889-895). Springer Netherlands.

34. Gil, J. M., Kim, S., & Lee, J. (2014). Task scheduling scheme based on resource clustering in desktop grids. International Journal of Communication Systems, 27(6), 918-930.

35. Great Internet Mersene Prime Search accessible from http://www.mersenne.org/

36. Hastie, T., Tibshirani, R., Friedman, J., (2008). The Elements of Statistical Learning. Springer.

37. Heien, E. M., Anderson, D. P., & Hagihara, K. (2009). Computing low latency batches with unreliable workers in volunteer computing environments .Journal of Grid Computing, 7(4), 501-518

38. HTCondor accessible from http://research.cs.wisc.edu/htcondor/

39. http://diggdata.in/post/94066544971/support-vector-machine-without-tears

40. http://documents.software.dell.com/Statistics/Textbook/Naive-Bayes-Classifier

41. http://neuralnetworksanddeeplearning.com/chap1.html

42. http://onlinestatbook.com/2/regression/intro.html

43. http://scikit-learn.org/stable/modules/naive_bayes.html

44. http://scikit-learn.org/stable/modules/svm.html

45. http://stattrek.com/regression/linear-regression.aspx

46. http://www.amazon.com/Predictive-Analytics-Power-Predict-Click/dp/1118356853

47. http://www.amazon.com/Predictive-Analytics-Power-Predict-Click/dp/1117434512

48. http://www.brighthub.com/environment/green-computing/articles/127086.aspx

49. http://www.cs.cmu.edu/~tom/mlbook.html

50. http://www.doc.ic.ac.uk/~nd/surprise_96/journal/vol4/cs11/report.html

51. http://www.ftpress.com/articles/article.aspx?p=2252409

52. http://www.ieeefinalyearprojects.org/Grid_computing_projects_in_java_dotnet.html

53. http://www.inf.ufrgs.br/~schnorr/download/publication/schnorr2012ccpe.pdf

54. http://www.insightexperts.nl/news-view/36542/data-mining-and-predictive-analytics.html

55. http://www.saedsayad.com/k_nearest_neighbors.htm

56. http://www.stat.yale.edu/Courses/1997-98/101/linreg.htm

57. http://www.statsoft.com/Textbook/Support-Vector-Machines

58. https://citizennet.com/blog/2012/11/10/random-forests-ensembles-and-performance-metrics/

59. https://en.wikipedia.org/wiki/Decision_tree

60. https://en.wikipedia.org/wiki/Naive_Bayes_classifier

61. https://mayuresha.wordpress.com/page/3/

62. https://rapidminer.com

63. https://www.r-project.org/

64. http://blog.revolutionanalytics.com/popularity/

65. https://source.ggy.bris.ac.uk/wiki/Data

66. https://statistics.laerd.com/spss-tutorials/linear-regression-using-spss-statistics.php

67. https://www.mindtools.com/dectree.html

68. https://www.quora.com/In-what-real-world-applications-is-Naive-Bayes-classifier-used

69. https://www.stat.berkeley.edu/~breiman/RandomForests/cc_home.htm

70. Huu, T. T., Koslovski, G., Anhalt, F., Montagnat, J., & Primet, P. V. B. (2011). Joint elastic cloud and virtual network framework for application performance-cost optimization. Journal of Grid Computing, 9(1), 27-47.

71. International Desktop Grid Federation, "Desktop Grid Applications", accessed from http://desktopgridfederation.org/applications.

72. Kang, W., Huang, H. H., & Grimshaw, A. (2013). Achieving high job execution reliability using underutilized resources in a computational economy. Future Generation Computer Systems, 29(3), 763-775.

73. Khan, M. K., Hyder, I., Chowdhry, B. S., Shafiq, F., & Ali, H. M. (2012). A novel fault tolerant volunteer selection mechanism for volunteer computing. Sindh University Research Journal—Science Series, 44(3), 138-143.

74. Klejnowski, L., Niemann, S., Bernard, Y., & Müller-Schloer, C. (2014). Using Trusted Communities to improve the speedup of agents in a Desktop Grid System. In Intelligent Distributed Computing VII (pp. 189-198). Springer International Publishing.

75. Kondo, D., Anderson, D. P., & McLeod, J. (2007, December). Performance evaluation of scheduling policies for volunteer computing. In e-Science and Grid Computing, IEEE International Conference on (pp. 415-422). IEEE.

76. Kondo, D., Araujo, F., Malecot, P., Domingues, P., Silva, L. M., Fedak, G., & Cappello, F. (2007). Characterizing result errors in internet desktop grids. In Euro-Par 2007 Parallel Processing (pp. 361-371). Springer Berlin Heidelberg

77. Kondo, D., Casanova, H., Wing, E., & Berman, F. (1993, October). Models and scheduling mechanisms for global computing applications. In Vehicle Navigation and Information Systems Conference, 1993., Proceedings of the IEEE-IEE (pp. 8-pp). IEEE.

78. Kondo, D., Chien, A. A., & Casanova, H. (2007). Scheduling task parallel applications for rapid turnaround on enterprise desktop grids. Journal of Grid Computing, 5(4), 379-405.

79. Kondo, D., Fedak, G., Cappello, F., Chien, A. A., & Casanova, H. (2006, December). On Resource Volatility in Enterprise Desktop Grids. In e-Science(p. 78).

80. Kondo, D., Javadi, B., Malecot, P., Cappello, F., & Anderson, D. P. (2009, May). Cost-benefit analysis of cloud computing versus desktop grids. In Parallel & Distributed Processing, 2009. IPDPS 2009. IEEE International Symposium on (pp. 1-12). IEEE.

81. Kondo, D., Taufer, M., Brooks III, C. L., Casanova, H., & Chien, A. (2004, April). Characterizing and evaluating desktop grids: An empirical study. In Parallel and Distributed Processing Symposium, 2004. Proceedings. 18th International (p. 26). IEEE

82. Krawczyk, S., & Bubendorfer, K. (2008, January). Grid resource allocation: allocation mechanisms and utilisation patterns. In Proceedings of the sixth Australasian workshop on Grid computing and e-research-Volume 82 (pp. 73-81). Australian Computer Society, Inc..

83. Lee, Y. C., Zomaya, A. Y., & Siegel, H. J. (2010). Robust task scheduling for volunteer computing systems. The Journal of Supercomputing, 53(1), 163-181.

84. Lerida, J. L., Solsona, F., Hernandez, P., Gine, F., Hanzich, M., & Conde, J. (2013). State-based predictions with self-correction on Enterprise Desktop Grid environments. Journal of Parallel and Distributed Computing, 73(6), 777-789.

85. Morrison, J. P., Kennedy, J. J., & Power, D. A. (2001). Webcom: A web based volunteer computer. The Journal of supercomputing, 18(1), 47-61

86. Mutka, M, H,. Linvy, M. (1987). Profiling workstations availabile capacity for remote execution. In Proc. 12 IFIPWG 7.3 Symposium on Computer Performance. 529-544

87. Mysteries for Protien Folding accessible from http://folding.stanford.edu/

88. Naseera, S., & Murthy, K. M. (2013). Prediction Based Job Scheduling Strategy for a Volunteer Desktop Grid. In Advances in Computing, Communication, and Control (pp. 25-38). Springer Berlin Heidelberg.

89. OurGrid accessible from http://www.ourgrid.org/

90. Pedroso, H., Silva, L. M., & Silva, J. G. (1997). Web-based metacomputing with JET. Concurrency: Practice and Experience, 9(11), 1169-1173.

91. Peng, D. T., & Shin, K. G. (1989, June). Static allocation of periodic tasks with precedence constraints in distributed real-time systems. In Distributed Computing Systems, 1989., 9th International Conference on (pp. 190-198). IEEE.

92. Peyvandi, S., Ahmad, R., & Zakaria, M. N. (2014). Scoring Model for Availability of Volatile Hosts in Volunteer Computing Environment. Journal of Theoretical & Applied Information Technology,70(2).

93. Platform Computing Inc. accessible from http://www. platform.com

94. Prabhu, C. S. R. (2008). Grid and Cluster Computing. PHI Learning Pvt. Ltd..

95. Rajaraman, V., & Murthy, C. S. R. (2008). Parallel computers: Architecture and programming. PHI Learning Pvt. Ltd..

96. Reddy, K. H. K., Roy, D. S., & Patra, M. R. (2014). A Comprehensive Performance Tuning Scheduling Framework for Computational Desktop Grid. International Journal of Grid and Distributed Computing, 7(1), 149-168.

97. Rood, B., & Lewis, M. J. (2010, May). Availability prediction based replication strategies for grid environments. In Cluster, Cloud and Grid Computing (CCGrid), 2010 10th IEEE/ACM International Conference on (pp. 25-33). IEEE

98. S. Chong,. How to track a user's idle time, accessible from http://www.codeproject.com/dll/trackuseridle.asp

99. S. Chong,. Idle tracking source code, accessible from http://www.codeproject.com/dll/TrackUserIdle/TrackUserIdle_src.zip

100. Salinas, S. A., Garino, C. G., & Zunino, A. (2012). An architecture for resource behavior prediction to improve scheduling systems performance on enterprise desktop grids. In Advances in New Technologies, Interactive Interfaces and Communicability (pp. 186-196). Springer Berlin Heidelberg.

101. Sarmenta, L. F. (2002). Sabotage-tolerance mechanisms for volunteer computing systems. Future Generation Computer Systems, 18(4), 561-572.

102. Sarmenta, L. F., & Hirano, S. (1999). Bayanihan: Building and studying web-based volunteer computing systems using Java. Future Generation Computer Systems, 15(5), 675-686.

103. Schulz, S., Blochinger, W., & Hannak, H. (2009). Capability-aware information aggregation in peer-to-peer Grids. Journal of Grid Computing,7(2), 135-167.

104. Search for Extraterrestrial Intelligence accesible from http:// setiathome.ssl.berkeley.edu/

105. Setia, S. K., Squillante, M. S., & Tripathi, S. K. (1994). Analysis of processor allocation in multiprogrammed, distributed-memory parallel processing systems. Parallel and Distributed Systems, IEEE Transactions on, 5(4), 401-420.

106. Shoch, J. F., & Hupp, J. A. (1982). The "worm" programs—early experience with a distributed computation. Communications of the ACM, 25(3), 172-180

107. Silaghi, G. C., Araujo, F., Silva, L. M., Domingues, P., & Arenas, A. E. (2009). Defeating colluding nodes in desktop grid computing platforms.Journal of Grid Computing, 7(4), 555-573

108. Sinha, P. K. (1998), Distributed Operating Systems: Concepts and Design, Prentice-Hall.

109. Sinha, P. K. (2002), Distributed Operating Systems: Concepts and Design, Prentice-Hall.

110. SZTAKI Desktop Grid, accessed from http://www.desktopgrid.hu/

111. Tanenbaum, A. S., & Van Steen, M. (2002). Distributed systems. Prentice-Hall.

112. Tchernykh, A., Pecero, J. E., Barrondo, A., & Schaeffer, E. (2014). Adaptive energy efficient scheduling in peer-to-peer desktop grids. Future Generation Computer Systems, 36, 209-220.

113. Toth, D., & Finkel, D. (2009). Improving the productivity of volunteer computing by using the most effective task retrieval policies. Journal of Grid Computing, 7(4), 519-535.

114. Villela, D. (2010). Minimizing the average completion time for concurrent Grid applications. Journal of Grid Computing, 8(1), 47-59.

115. Vlădoiu, M. (2010). Has Open Source Prevailed in Desktop Grid and Volunteer Computing?. Petroleum-Gas University of Ploiesti Bulletin, Mathematics-Informatics-Physics Series, 62(2).

116. Watanabe, K., Fukushi, M., & Horiguchi, S. (2009). Optimal spot-checking for computation time minimization in volunteer computing. Journal of Grid Computing, 7(4), 575-600.

117. Watts, J., & Taylor, S. (1998). A practical approach to dynamic load balancing. Parallel and Distributed Systems, IEEE Transactions on, 9(3), 235-248.

118. Xavier, E. C., Peixoto, R. R., & da Silveira, J. L. (2013). Scheduling with task replication on desktop grids: theoretical and experimental analysis .Journal of Combinatorial Optimization, 1-25.

119. XtremeWeb accessible from http://www.xtremweb.net/

120. Yang, C. T., Leu, F. Y., & Chen, S. Y. (2010). Network Bandwidth-aware job scheduling with dynamic information model for Grid resource brokers. The Journal of Supercomputing, 52(3), 199-223.

121. Zhao, Y., Chen, L., Li, Y., Liu, P., Li, X., & Zhu, C. (2013). RAS: A Task Scheduling Algorithm Based on Resource Attribute Selection in a Task Scheduling Framework. In Internet and Distributed Computing Systems (pp. 106-119). Springer Berlin Heidelberg.